THE 21ST CENTURY INVESTOR

INVESTING for YOUR CHILD'S COLLEGE EDUCATION

THE 21ST CENTURY INVESTOR

INVESTING for YOUR CHILD'S COLLEGE EDUCATION

MIKE POWERS

A Third Millennium Press Book

AVON BOOKS NEW YORK

AVON BOOKS, INC.
1350 Avenue of the Americas
New York, New York 10019

Front cover illustration by Devaney Stock Photos, Inc.
Visit our website at **http://www.AvonBooks.com**
ISBN: 0-380-79064-5

Library of Congress Cataloging in Publication Data:

Powers, Mike.
The 21st century investor : investing for your child's college education / Mike Powers.
p. cm.
Includes bibliographical references and index.
1. Student aid—United States. 2. College costs—United States. 3. Parents—United States—Finance, Personal. 4. Investments—United States. I. Title.
LB2337.4.P69 1998 98-24671
378.3'8—dc21 CIP

First Avon Books Trade Paperback Printing: November 1998

Printed in the U.S.A.

OPM 10 9 8 7 6 5 4 3 2 1

ACKNOWLEDGMENTS

Thanks to Mark Levine and Deirdre Martin for their friendship and good company (even if they are Ranger fans), and to Stephen Pollan and Stuart Krichevsky for their advice and support. And special thanks and love to my wife, Jacquie, and my children, Jenneka and Alex, for making this an exceptionally good life.

CONTENTS

THE 21ST CENTURY INVESTOR

INVESTING *for* YOUR CHILD'S COLLEGE EDUCATION

1

THE BIGGEST INVESTMENT YOU'LL EVER MAKE?

If you have children, or are even thinking about having children, you need to read this book. It will help you prepare for what is becoming the biggest financial hurdle (and horror) for the average American family—paying for a college education.

For most people, the cost of sending a child to college will represent, next to their homes, the biggest investment they'll ever make. For those who send their children to an Ivy League school or one of the country's other leading private institutions, the cost may well exceed the value of their homes.

As this book was being written, a year of undergraduate education in the private colleges at Cornell University, the largest of the Ivies, was $29,489, including tuition, fees, room and board, books, and miscellaneous expenses. (Some of Cornell's colleges are part of the State University of New York system and have lower tuition.) Assuming a conservative 5 percent annual increase, the final bill will total just over $127,000. Adding in money for travel, clothing, and other incidentals, it will easily top $130,000.

Perhaps the best way to look at how college costs have increased is to compare them to the rate of inflation and the costs of some other common big-ticket items. According to the Bureau of Labor Statistics, inflation has increased 80 percent since 1980. During the same period, the average cost of a new car has risen only 54 percent, which is a surprise, and the cost of medical care has risen 182 percent, which is not a surprise.

But college tuition? It's left even medical care in the dust with a whopping 253 percent increase, more than three times the rate of inflation. The cost of the average private college now absorbs nearly 50 percent of the median American family's household income.

But it's not just the nation's elite private colleges that have skyrocketed in cost. Consider state-supported public schools, which for years have been the backbone of higher education with their promise of a good education at a reasonable price. Even these "affordable" institutions will put a painful dent in most families' pocketbooks. The average bill for four years at a state college is now around $40,000. And in recent years their prices have been increasing almost as fast as those of private colleges. At Cornell in 1996–97, the state colleges charged New York State residents $17,389. Applying the same 5 percent annual increase we used for Cornell's private colleges, that comes out to almost $75,000 for a four-year stint.

WHY HAS COLLEGE BECOME SO EXPENSIVE?

Good question. Until around 1980, the cost of attending college had always increased at roughly the rate of inflation. Since then, it's increased at a rate more than triple that of inflation. But why?

On March 31, 1996, the *Philadelphia Inquirer* published the first article in a multipart series that tried to answer this question. Its conclusion? Colleges have become top-heavy bureaucratic quagmires, where dollars are gobbled up by administrative costs and not by instruction. The article pointed out that since 1973, while the nation's undergraduate population has grown by 28 percent, its teaching faculties have increased only 22 percent. At the same time, the number of nonteaching administrators and staff has increased 83 percent.

For a particularly appalling example, the paper needed to look no further than its crosstown neighbor, the University of Pennsylvania. Good school—Ivy League, in fact—with a long history of acclaimed educational programs, including one of the country's premier business schools, and an impressive list of prominent alumni. But the reporters who wrote the series found an interesting fact during their research. In 1996, they discovered, there were 29 more students registered at Penn than there had been in 1980. When they looked at the number of nonteaching administrators and staff, however, they found that this population of paper shufflers and keyboard tappers had increased by 1,820! That's 63 new employees for every new student!

Who are all these people crowding the nation's campuses? Some are administrators hired to assist higher-level administrators. Where there's a president or a provost, you'll be sure to find an executive vice president, a half dozen or so vice presidents and vice provosts, a smattering of associate and assistant vice presidents and vice provosts, a few deputy vice presidents or vice provosts, and a whole bunch of administrative assistants to keep them from bumping into each other. It's like a Dilbert cartoon come to life.

Colleges and universities have also become prisoners of technology. The popularity of computers, and more recently the Internet and World Wide Web, has required most schools to hire an army of technicians to operate the huge campuswide networks they've installed in recent years. They've needed new staff to run the recreation and dining facilities that make many campuses seem more like resorts than schools. They've beefed up their development offices to generate more and more gifts. And because they have all these new people on their payrolls, they've had to increase the size of their human resources staffs.

THEY HAVE PLENTY OF MONEY—WHY DO THEY WANT SO MUCH OF OURS?

When you look at the way colleges and universities operate, it's hard to imagine why they need to keep increasing tuition. First of all, they're nonprofit institutions and are exempt from taxes. Plus they get federal and state support.

They're also masters at fund-raising, and they collect billions of dollars in gifts every year. Most of this money goes to their endowments. These are huge chunks of cash—trust funds, really—that get invested in a wide variety of places. (Some of these are surprisingly risky. I once worked for a stock options brokerage firm on the Philadelphia Stock Exchange. One of our clients traded with Harvard endowment money. It's not a route most investment counselors would consider conservative.) The money generated by their investments is put toward operating costs, student aid, research, or plowed back into the endowment. As with any well-managed trust fund, the endowment principal itself remains untouched.

If you take a look at the colleges and universities with the biggest endowments, you'll find they're also the institutions with the highest tuitions. Harvard, for example, has the nation's largest endowment—$6.2 billion. It also charges its students $28,896 a year. Princeton? Number four in endowment and a $28,725 price tag. Stanford? Number five in endowment and $27,830 a year. MIT? Number ten and $28,350.

Where does all this money go? A lot of it pays for infrastructure like constructing new buildings and refurbishing old ones, keeping streets and parking lots in good shape, wiring entire campuses and purchasing hardware and software to keep up with the latest electronic technologies. The biggest universities are like small cities, with their own governments and their own police forces. Many operate their own utility and phone systems. Just maintaining the grounds on a several-hundred-acre campus can cost millions of dollars a year.

A lot of the money goes for scholarships and financial aid, too. Despite the top-heavy administrative bloating that plagues most schools today, their hearts are in the right place. They go out of their way to make education available to all students, regardless of their economic situation. As a result, those who can pay end up paying more so that those who can't pay can still get an education. (In the second part of this book we'll take a look at how you and your child can take advantage of scholarships and other financial aid opportunities.)

But, unfortunately, the inescapable bottom line with colleges and universities is that there is no bottom line. They don't make money, they spend it. They don't operate like businesses, whose every waking moment is driven by the need to operate as efficiently as possible to maximize profits. Rather, they dole out the income they receive from tuition and gifts and endowment and other sources to administrators whose sole job is to make sure they don't overrun their budgets. And most of those administrators are academics themselves, whose money managing skills have been honed by on-the-job training within academia, not in the business world. It's a system that does not generate fiscal effectiveness. If universities were businesses, most would be out of business.

WHY DO WE CONTINUE TO PAY THE PRICE?

College costs don't follow the normal laws of economics. Since the baby boom generation graduated, applications for admission to undergraduate programs have actually gone down. If we apply basic supply and demand economic theory to the situation, the price of college should have dropped as institutions competed with one another for the best students.

Instead, the opposite has happened. And for one simple reason that also has to do with economics: a college degree means more earning power. In recent years, as work in the United States has moved from being manufacturing-based to technology- and service-based, the market for semiskilled labor has dropped through the floor. As a result, the need for a college education has never been greater. The average high school dropout makes around $11,000 a year. A high school diploma will get you an average of about $17,000 a year. But a bachelor's degree jumps average income up to nearly $30,000 a year. Graduate and professional degrees increase it even further.

So what we're buying our children with our expensive college tuition payments is the ability to get a good job and make more money over the course of their lifetimes. Without it, they're headed for 50 years of wearing funny little paper hats and endlessly repeating, "Would you like fries with that?" We know this, and we'll pay whatever it costs to help them avoid it.

Colleges and universities know it, too. So they've gone out of their way to make themselves as appealing as possible. This costs money, and many critics of higher education argue that all the extra money charged by colleges and universities over the last 15 years has been spent more on style than substance. The fact that teaching faculties have not kept pace with the increase in enrollments is certainly hard evidence of this, as is the outlandish increase in staff and administration.

In effect, the critics argue, colleges have been conducting the institutional equivalent of the Miss America pageant, trying their damnedest to spruce up their images to attract more students. And they're not doing it by improving instruction or hiring more faculty. They're doing it by constructing more buildings and hiring more administrative staff and building more tennis courts and throwing more money at—let's all pause for a moment of reverential silence—research.

Ah, yes. Research. Is there any institution that admires or glorifies itself more than the research university? The nation's finest minds locked in fierce intellectual battle with the most pressing problems of the day, they tell us. Who wouldn't want their child studying in the midst of such noble endeavors? This approach has proven to be a very effective marketing tool for quite a few of the biggest schools. Twenty percent of the nation's college students are enrolled at research universities.

To a degree, they're right. Research universities do offer students opportunities that smaller schools don't. And some of the work that goes on is absolutely astonishing and will no doubt provide enormous benefits to society. But a lot of it is redundant and downright silly. When you've sat at a table full of professors and heard one say to another something like, "Well, I just completed a comprehensive three-year study that clearly shows a distinct correlation between educational attainment and workforce participation," you can't help but be a little cynical.

"Gee, you mean you need to go to school to get a decent job? Tell me something I don't know, Einstein," you want to scream. "And someone actually gave you money to figure this out?"

But for every hundred self-important assistant professors trying desperately to get published and avoid falling off the tenure track, there are one or two true stars of international acclaim who research universities love to show off to potential students and their families. The problem is these stars are usually far removed from teaching and campus life in general. A student can spend his entire four-year career without ever laying eyes on the person whose presence on the faculty enticed him to enroll in the first place.

In the meantime, the average faculty member is so absorbed with applying for research grants and submitting papers to journals for publication that teaching takes a back seat. And often it's way in the back. Talk to a professor at a research university sometime. They can talk for hours about the agony of writing grant proposals and the rigor of conducting their research projects, but when it comes to teaching, it's frequently hard to carry on much of a conversation.

The emphasis on research can be seen in the reduction of teaching hours. Twenty years ago, professors taught 12 to 15 hours a week. Today, according to Department of Education statistics, a third of all professors at research universities average fewer than four hours a week teaching students. More than 40 percent of teachers at private research universities teach just a single course a semester. To make up the slack, their institutions hire more junior faculty and administrators to carry out teaching and advising tasks. In turn, this increases costs.

DO WE GET WHAT WE PAY FOR?

It depends on how you look at it. We as consumers have come to believe that the value of a college education is directly related to its cost and the prestige of the college or university whose name we write on our checks. Most of us would love to have our children attend a Yale or a Swarthmore or a Stanford. Why? Because we've been brainwashed into thinking the educations they offer are far superior to those of other colleges and universities. That, and the fact that we love having their decals on the rear windows of our cars.

This is not to say these schools don't provide good educations. They do. But so do a lot of other schools that don't have the glossy patina that accompanies the Ivy League and the other elite schools. I recently sat in the office of a concerned professor at an Ivy League university who worried whether the price of attending a school like hers is worth it anymore. The product of a state university in the Midwest, she frankly questioned whether the undergraduate education students receive where she teaches is three times as good as the education offered by her alma mater. If you compare their current costs, she pointed out, it should be.

Is it? Of course not. But is it three times as prestigious? Yes, without question. And will it open more doors with employers when the sheepskins have been handed out? Yes, at least that's what we've been led to believe. And is there a network of successful and influential alumni to hit on when that time comes? Most definitely. And will it provide a better income over the course of the graduates' lives? Quite possibly. So if you measure the expense of college by the same measure as you would an investment, the return on investment may be worth it. It depends on the field your child enters as much as anything else.

So that's what college has come down to for a lot of people: prestige and, hopefully, wealth down the line. This is why a college education will continue to become more and more expensive and why we'll continue to cough up the bucks to pay for it.

WHAT'S NEXT?

Unfortunately, nothing you or I can do is going to make higher education any cheaper. College costs have been on an upward spiral for more than 15 years now. The rate of increase may slow down somewhat, but unless colleges finally begin to experience a decline in customers, there's little reason to believe the trend will change very much. You might as well bite the bullet and get ready to pay.

This book will help you get ready. In chapter 2 we'll discuss what kind of college or university might be right for your child. Not everyone is Ivy League material, after all. In fact, you may find that the local community college fits your needs perfectly. We'll also look at some students from a variety of high schools and educational and socioeconomic backgrounds to see what kinds of schools are right for them.

The rest of the book is divided into two sections called Paying the Bills, Parts 1 and 2. Part 1 discusses the various investment options you can use as part of your college payment strategy. We'll look at common investment vehicles like stocks, bonds, and mutual funds. We'll talk a bit about more exotic and high-risk strategies like futures and options. We'll also examine real estate and life insurance.

Part 2 looks at the many financial aid resources you can pursue to pay for college. We'll begin by looking at how financial aid officers look at you and how you can position yourself to qualify for as much financial aid as possible. Then we'll investigate how you can tap into the billions of dollars in financial aid that are made available to students every year, including grants and scholarships. You'll be amazed at how many there are and how many go unclaimed. Your child's academic skill, athletic prowess, or other talents might just land one.

Women and minorities have many financial aid options these days, and Part 2 includes a list of some of the best opportunities. In recent years more and more states have begun offering a program that lets you prepay your child's tuition at current rates. It's a great way to save on college costs, but there are downsides. We'll discuss the positives and the negatives of prepaid tuition.

Many students contribute to college costs by holding down part-time jobs, quite a few of which are available through college work-study programs. We'll look at these and other ways your child can help foot the bills. We'll also look at the last resort—loans. They're an inescapable fact of life for many families with children headed to college, but they don't have to break you. We'll look at the most common sources, and a few uncommon ones, too.

When you've finished the book, you'll have learned that college doesn't have to break the bank. If you start preparing early, take advantage of the investment strategies outlined in Part 1, and research the many opportunities for financial assistance discussed in Part 2, no college or university should be beyond your reach.

2

WHAT COLLEGES ARE RIGHT FOR YOUR CHILD?

If you found the first chapter of this book frightening, let me console you a bit. Not every college in the United States will require you to mortgage your house and car and sell your dog just to meet tuition and room and board costs. There are roughly 3,000 colleges and universities in the United States, and their costs vary greatly, ranging from expensive Ivy League universities to moderately priced state universities to downright affordable local community colleges. Your child's talents and goals will determine how expensive a school he or she might attend. This chapter looks at some factors to consider when the two of you begin the difficult search for the ''right'' school.

AN IMPORTANT NOTE TO PARENTS

Your son or daughter is the one going to college, not you, and he or she must make the final decision. This is one of the hardest things for many parents to remember when their child is going through college selection. College is the first step in letting go, and the search and application process is part of that separation.

You'll be tempted to try to control things and influence your child's choices. It's only natural. And while it's okay to have opinions, you must make sure your opinions don't become demands. Some parents get so carried away they end up filling out all the application forms and even writing the essay.

The rest of this chapter has been written for your college-bound child. However, you *both* need to read it and use it as a starting point for discussion. When you've finished, step back and let your child choose his or her own path.

GETTING STARTED

High school graduation is on the horizon, and it's time to decide where you'll attend college. It will more than likely be the most nerve-racking decision you've faced in your 17 or 18 years. It's an enormous step toward preparing yourself for a life of constructive and rewarding work. But before you begin to look for the right college, you need to take a hard look at yourself, your needs, your goals, and the things that make you happiest.

This may not be an easy task. You'll probably end up asking questions of yourself that you've never asked before. Be honest, write down your answers, and when you've finished, use them to help you through the decision-making process.

What Size School Is Right for You?

You're going to be picking from among colleges and universities that range in size from a few hundred to tens of thousands of students. More than 80 percent of the private colleges in this country have fewer than 2,500 students. On the other hand, 75 percent of the nation's public universities have enrollments of more than 2,500 students. Some of the largest, like Arizona State and Ohio State, have more than 30,000.

Generally, smaller schools offer smaller class sizes. Teaching—not research—is given greater emphasis at small schools. Classes tend to be organized more around discussions than lectures, so you'll find you have a lot of one-on-one interaction with your professors. You'll also be more likely to develop friendships with them outside of class.

Smaller schools offer more of a sense of community than large universities do. Everyone gets to know everyone else to some degree. Extracurricular activities tend to involve a greater portion of the student population. There's less competition for resources. The library is less crowded, and computer facilities are more accessible. It's also easier to get the help you need if you have academic or personal problems.

Don't get me wrong: there are also many benefits to larger colleges and universities. They have more course offerings, so you can study subjects in many different fields. If you're undecided about a career, such a broad range of offerings lets you explore different options.

Large schools also have more resources—bigger and better labs, more sophisticated computer networks, more athletic facilities and intramural sports programs bigger libraries, and increased opportunities for off-campus study like semester abroad programs and internships. Although many required courses have large class sizes and may even be run by teaching assistants, higher-level courses usually have smaller enrollments and present excellent opportunities for interaction with professors.

What Kind of Academic Offerings Are You Looking For?

You need to chose between a liberal arts curriculum and a more specialized program with intense concentration in a certain field. Liberal arts curriculums offer you a broad range of courses in the humanities (like English, languages, philosophy, art, and music), the hard sciences (like math, biology, and chemistry), and the social sciences (like psychology, history, economics, and sociology). Most students will take a range of courses during their first and second years and then declare a major area of study by their third year. A liberal arts background is excellent preparation for graduate school or professional training in law school, medical school, or business school.

A more specialized program will prepare you for immediate entry after graduation into either a profession (like engineering or teaching) or business. Most large universities have colleges devoted to these fields. They offer four-year curriculums with a greater emphasis on a subject than you will find in a liberal arts curriculum.

What Kind of Academic Environment Do You Prefer?

One simple fact of college life is that some colleges and universities are more academically rigorous than others. The hardest schools challenge their students with workloads and expectations that few have ever experienced before. Achieving good grades requires discipline, organization, and a lot of plain hard work. Other schools put less academic pressure on their students, and earning decent grades requires less effort.

It's extremely important that you be honest with yourself in answering this question. If you want to get all you can out of college academically and intellectually, then a school with a tough academic reputation may be right for you. But if you're interested in a balance of school work, social events, and other activities, you might be happier at a school with less pressure.

You also need to be realistic about your own capabilities and work habits. Are you organized, or is your life a mess? Do you keep up with work, or are you a procrastinator? If you've managed to get good grades in high school with little effort, the same amount of effort is not going to do the trick at an academically challenging school. Can you pull it up a notch or two, or are you likely to maintain the same work habits? Your answers to these questions will determine what kind of school you should attend.

On the other hand, don't sell yourself short. College should be a time of new challenges. Many students who coasted through high school find—usually to their own surprise and delight—that they have the discipline and willpower to excel when challenged with a difficult curriculum. It's all a part of growing up and learning more about yourself.

Do You Prefer a Coeducational or Single-sex Campus?

Many students are surprised to learn there are still single-sex colleges in the United States. Most are for women, and for some women they're the perfect environment.

A close friend of mine attended a women's college in Virginia in the early '70s and loved it. During the week, without the distraction of men and all the baggage that accompanies relationships between the sexes, she found it much easier to concentrate on her studies. On weekends, men from nearby colleges would visit, or she and her friends would go to their campuses. She thoroughly enjoyed her four years at the school and says she honestly never felt like she was missing anything by not attending a coed school.

My friend's experience is not unusual. Women who attend all-women colleges generally become more interested in their courses, have more confidence in their intellectual abilities, and go on to graduate school more often than women in coeducational schools.

What Region of the Country Do You Want to Be In?

One of the neat things about picking a college is that it's kind of like planning a vacation. Where do you want to go? Some students prefer to remain close enough to home that they can visit on weekends if they choose. Others are anxious to move to a completely new area and experience new weather patterns and geography and lifestyles.

Keep in mind that the further away you move for school, the more difficult and expensive it will be for you and your parents to travel back and forth. If you're already cutting it close financially, staying nearby to eliminate travel costs is probably an excellent idea.

Do You Prefer an Urban, Surburban, or Rural Environment?

What's it going to be—the city, the 'burbs, or the sticks? Your environment will have a significant effect on your lifestyle and general happiness with college life.

City life can be great for many students. You'll certainly have more options when it comes to activities away from campus. But it's also noisy and expensive, and you'll have certain safety issues to think about. You may also find that due to crowding and the general expense of land, some city schools may not have some of the facilities that are important to you.

If you want to be near a city but not have to deal with hassles of urban life, a suburban school might be the ticket. You'll have plenty of access to shopping and theaters and restaurants. You'll also find that suburban campuses are larger and frequently have more facilities than those in cities. And if you want to head into town, it's a short trip that can usually be accomplished on public transportation.

The other end of the spectrum is attending a school in a small town or rural location. This will offer you a quieter environment with fewer distractions. Many students find the quality of life better in this type of environment. The lack of distractions is often more conducive to study. It also fosters a sense of community on campus. And sometimes you can have the best of both worlds. If you like what cities have to offer, many "rural" campuses are only an hour or two from some of the nation's major metropolitan areas.

Do You Prefer a College with a Certain Religious or Ethnic Affiliation?

Some colleges are tied to a certain religious denomination or have a student population that's largely made up of a certain ethnic group. Among schools affiliated with a religious group, there is considerable variation in the degree of religious influence. Some require attendance at services and religion classes and have strict rules governing dress and conduct. At others religion may have little effect on day-to-day campus life.

Schools with certain ethnic affiliations may benefit minorities such as African Americans, Asians, or Hispanics. The chance to interact with role models and the networks of successful alumni offered by these schools are often useful to minority students. Many are also more comfortable being part of the majority ethnic population on campus than feeling isolated at a school with a predominantly Caucasian population.

Do You Want a School Where Fraternities and Sororities Are Active?

After a decline in popularity in the '70s and '80s, fraternities and sororities are on the rebound. Greek life dominates the social scene at some colleges and universities. At others, it's of less importance. For students who like being a part of a larger group and being in the middle of lots of activities, fraternity and sorority life is often a wonderful part of the college experience. For students who tend to go their own way, they are usually of little importance.

Keep in mind that there is more to Greek life than parties. Each house has its own personality, and many are active with community organizations or are involved in other public service activities. And Greeks also study. In fact, at many schools the average GPA of fraternity and sorority members is higher than that of the rest of the student population.

What Nonacademic Activities Are You Looking For?

Don't evaluate a college or university solely on its academic offerings. You're going to want to have some fun when you're finished studying, so you'll want to make sure the school you select has the activities you like.

For many high school athletes who don't go on to play varsity sports in college, an active intramural sports program is absolutely essential. Perhaps you're a musician and would like to play in a band or orchestra. Maybe you're into theater and would like to join a theater group. Think about the things you like to do, or would like to learn to do, and make sure they're offered at the schools you're considering.

How Will the Availability of Financial Aid Affect Your Choice?

You and your parents need to work closely on this one. Sit down together and figure out exactly how much they can afford for each year of college. Then factor in your own contribution from summer jobs or working during the school year. This will give you some idea of how much extra you'll need to get through a year at each college you're considering.

Don't get discouraged by hefty price tags. Very few students today come from families who can afford the entire price tag of a four-year education. As you'll see later in this book, there are an astounding number of sources for scholarships and financial aid in this country. And plenty of students take advantage of them.

How Do You Stack Up Academically Against the Competition?

Take a look at your academic achievements. Write down your grade point average, SAT or ACT scores, and class rank. You can use these to compare yourself with students already attending the schools you're interested in. Hopefully, you'll find that your grades and test scores fall within (or even a little above) their range. On the other hand, you also might find that some schools are a bit more academically demanding than you're prepared to handle. You might as well figure it out ahead of time and save the application fee.

What Are Your Career Goals?

Finally, evaluate your career goals. I know this is a huge and intimidating gray area for many high school juniors and seniors, but don't worry about it. It's perfectly normal to be undecided at this age about what you want to do. If you do know, you're that much ahead of the game. If you don't, you probably at least have areas of interest that may turn into career options. Keep them in mind when you're evaluating different schools.

THE RESEARCH PROCESS

Once you've analyzed your own qualities and the qualities you're looking for in a college, it's time to start your research. Take your time, and be thorough. You're not just planning for the next four years, you're making a decision that could have a big influence on the rest of your life.

Here are your best sources for information.

Your guidance counselor.

Your first and best resource will be your high school guidance counselor. His job is to help you find schools that match your interests, goals, and talents. Share with him the information you learned about yourself in the previous section of this chapter. Be frank, express your concerns, and listen to what he has to say.

Outside counselors.

Independent college counselors are doing a land office business these days. For some parents, particularly those with deep pockets, no expense is too great if they think it'll get their child into the right school.

Are these counselors worth the money they charge (as much as $1,000)? It depends. If the college counseling resources at your high school are poor, or if you feel your counselor is simply overburdened with too many students to give everyone enough attention, they might be. My advice is to work with your high school staff first. If you feel you're not getting the information you need, then start looking for an independent.

Two good sources of independent counselors are the National Association for College Admission Counseling (703-836-2222) and the Independent Educational Consultants Association (703-591-4850). Make sure their services and fees are explained thoroughly before you hire them. And if you run into counselors who guarantee they can get you into a particular school, thank them politely and walk away—fast.

College representatives.

Most colleges have admissions officers who spend a significant portion of the year traveling around the country to meet with high school students and their parents. They often are recent graduates of the colleges they represent, and they do an excellent job of describing what their schools have to offer. They're also able to answer just about any question you can throw at them.

Alumni.

As any college officer will tell you, alumni are a college's best ambassadors. Like college representatives, they'll give you the inside dirt on campus life, different majors, the faculty, and other information. The downside is you'll find alumni of varying ages, and the longer they've been away from school, the less accurate their knowledge will be. The younger they are, the more accurate the report you'll get.

Friends.

Friends attending college are also excellent sources of information. Not only can they give you the picture of a school from the inside but they'll also be more likely to show the negatives than either college representatives or alumni will.

Guidebooks.

There are dozens of college guidebooks on the market, ranging from unbiased, carefully researched publications that are careful to remain neutral to more subjective publications that are fond of making endless lists of the "best" this and the "best" that.

College recruiting material.

Colleges and universities go to great pains—and expense—to create handsome and informative materials to send to prospective students. They're very thorough and can guide you step-by-step through the application process. Most schools today also have sites on the World Wide Web.

PREPARING YOUR PRELIMINARY LIST

After you've completed your research, you'll have three tasks before you: making a list of potential candidates, choosing the ones to which you'll apply, and deciding which one you'll attend.

Start by writing down every college or university that's ever interested you. It doesn't cost anything, so if a school sounds interesting, put it on your list. You'll have learned about some schools through your high school's guidance office and the other resources you've consulted. You may have developed awareness of others through friends or acquaintances who attend them. Most students have an interest in the schools their parents attended. Maybe you like a certain school's football team or basketball team. You may have even learned of some through television. Bill Cosby and Jerry Seinfeld have probably given their alma maters (Temple University and Queens College, respectively) more exposure through their television shows and personal celebrity than either school ever received through conventional public relations strategies.

NARROWING YOUR CHOICES

Once you've completed your list, it's time for a hard evaluation. You've already determined the qualities you're looking for in a college. Use them to evaluate each of your candidates. Remove schools that aren't in your desired geographic area or that are too big or too small. If a school doesn't have the academic and extracurricular programs you're interested in, knock it off the list. If you find you just don't match up academically against the students who go to a school, you should probably cross it off.

When you've finished, you may end up with eight or ten candidates. Or you may only have two or three. There are no rules on how many schools you should actually apply to. But be sure your final choices meet your criteria, and be realistic about your chances for acceptance. For example, if you're a C student with combined SAT scores of 1,000, don't bother sending an application to Princeton or Yale or Harvard. There are better ways to waste $75. That leads us to the next topic.

SHOULD YOU APPLY FOR EARLY DECISION?

Many students think that applying for early admission increases their chances of being accepted.

True? In some cases, it probably is. In fact, despite their claims to the contrary, the acceptance histories of many of the nation's most prestigious colleges and universities show a higher acceptance rate among early decision candidates than among regular candidates. Princeton, for instance, accepts more than 35 percent of its early decision applicants but less than 10 percent of its regular applicants. Early acceptance is a binding commitment on the part of the applicant, so for colleges it's a way of locking in customers. Unless you can demonstrate extraordinary circumstances, such as not being completely aware of the financial requirements of attending a school, most schools will hold you to your commitment.

Is it a good move? Yes, but only if you're absolutely certain you've picked the right school. And don't think you can get away with applying for early decision to more than one school. College admissions offices compare notes with their competition on early decision applicants. If your name should show up on more than one list, you'll be warned that you have to withdraw your applications from all but one school. In a worst-case scenario, you run the risk of being denied early admission to all the schools you've applied to. Fortunately, most guidance counselors are well aware of the problems associated with multiple early decision applications and will prevent you from making this mistake.

There's one good reason not to apply for early decision. Students who are looking for substantial financial aid may find that early decision is against their best interests. First of all, since they've made a commitment to the school, they're going to have to accept whatever financial aid package they're offered. And some schools have been accused of cutting back on financial aid to early decision applicants for this very reason. Most students are probably better off going the regular application route so they're able to compare financial aid packages.

THE SAFETY SCHOOL

The safety school is the insurance policy of the college application process. While it's certainly admirable to set your sights high and apply to the best schools you can find, you don't want to find your mailbox jammed with nothing but rejection notices in the spring.

This is where the safety school comes into play. Pick at least one college that you know you'll be able to get into. Many students will send in an application to their state university, for example. It may not be your first choice, but it'll keep you from finding yourself working the graveyard shift at your local 7-Eleven next fall.

VISITING CAMPUSES

If at all possible, you should visit as many of the colleges and universities on your final list as you can. Catalogs and guidebooks and college representatives will certainly give you excellent information about their schools. But the best way to get a complete picture is to visit a school for a day or so. The best time to visit is early in the fall of your senior year. While a summer visit between your junior and senior year is probably more convenient to your family's schedule, you'll usually find most campuses on downtime with most of the students away and only summer courses in session.

Plan on spending at least a day at each school. If you can, stay overnight on campus. Take the official guided tour (remember to call ahead to check the schedules and make an appointment), and then wander around on your own. Make sure you check out the college or department you might be studying in. If you can find a large lecture class, go in and take a seat for a while. Poke your head into some labs, and visit the student union. Check out the dining halls and dormitories. And don't be shy. Although you'll feel conspicuous and out-of-place, you'll actually blend right in. Remember, at least a quarter of the kids on that campus are only a year older than you.

THE INTERVIEW

Some students arrange to have an interview with an admissions officer when they're visiting a campus. Again, it's a good way to learn more about the school. Use the opportunity to double-check the information you've received from your high school counselor and other sources. Make a list of questions beforehand, and make sure they all get answered. Be prepared to answer some questions, too. The admissions officer will be just as interested in you as you are about the college.

If you can arrange it, an interview with a professor in the area in which you intend to study is a good idea. They can give you information about course expectations, explain the course sequences you'll need to earn a degree, give you an idea of the workload you can expect, explain testing and grading procedures, discuss opportunities for undergraduate research and off-campus study programs, and tell you about the careers of recent graduates.

THE APPLICATION

The final step in the process is filling out an application for each of your final candidates and sending them off with a check. Then you wait. But at least you're almost finished with the admissions process.

As for the check writing process, that never really ends. Starting with your application fee, you may spend the rest of your life writing checks to your college. While you're a student, they're for tuition. But after you graduate? Well, remember the development people I mentioned in the first chapter? They'll always know where you are, and their hands will always be out.

MAKING THE MATCH—EIGHT STUDENTS AND THEIR COLLEGE OPTIONS

The following eight students are all on their way to college. They represent a variety of academic capabilities, interests, talents, goals, and family backgrounds. Each will pursue a path quite different from the others. With one exception, they're all unsure about what they want to do in life. They also each have different expectations for college. By reading about their lives, their high school performances, and their college choices, you may be able to get a feel for the path you should follow.

Aaron

Aaron attends a public high school in a suburb of Cleveland. He's an above-average student with a grade point average of 2.95 and SAT scores of 570 in math and 510 in verbal. He ranks in the top quarter of his high school class.

Aaron is one of the most popular students in his school and is an avid athlete. He has lettered three years in both football and baseball and, although he has neither the size nor the talent to be a Division I prospect, hopes to play one or both sports in college. He also helped organize and referees in a youth basketball league. He's a member of the student government and is involved in several school organizations.

Aaron has worked part-time in a computer store for the last two years and has developed an interest in business. He also has an interest in journalism and has given thought to becoming a newspaper sportswriter. He has visited large state universities in

Ohio and Pennsylvania and was a bit intimidated by their size, so he's come to the conclusion he'd be happier at a smaller school. Although he's looking forward to going away to school, he prefers to remain within an easy drive of home.

Aaron's parents both work. His father is a real estate broker, and his mother is an administrative aide at his high school. Their combined annual income is around $85,000. In addition to Aaron, they have two younger daughters they'll need to put through school. They will be making their decision on where Aaron will attend college in part on financial aid offerings.

Aaron's options

Aaron's desire to participate in sports and his desire to go to a smaller school not too far from home point to a Division III school in the Midwest, or Northeast. The College of Wooster, Wittenburg University, and Ohio Wesleyan University, all in Ohio, would fill all three requirements. Other good prospects in nearby states include Franklin and Marshall College, Washington and Jefferson College and Dickinson College in Pennsylvania; DePauw University and Earlham College in Indiana; and St. Bonaventure University and Canisius College in New York.

Suzanne

Suzanne is an admissions officer's dream. She attends a suburban high school outside San Diego and is one of the three or four top students in her class. Her GPA is 3.95, her SATs are 760 in math and 750 in verbal, and she's a member of the National Honor Society and a National Merit Scholar finalist. She plays soccer and lacrosse, is editor of the high school yearbook, and participates in student council and many other school activities.

Suzanne is relatively rare among high school students in that she has firm career plans. She has known since she was 15 that she wants to be an attorney specializing in civil liberties issues. She has already decided she wants to go to Harvard Law School. Now she has to figure out which undergraduate program will get her there. She likes the idea of attending an Ivy League school but hates the idea of being so far away from home. But she's very practical and focused and will base her decision on what's best for her career plans.

Suzanne's father is an airline pilot, and her mother is a publications editor at a local college. Their combined annual income is around $125,000, and they have twin boys four years younger than Suzanne. They're already worried about putting them all through school, particularly if they all decide to pursue graduate or professional degrees. Suzanne will apply for financial aid and hopes that her academic accomplishments will win her a scholarship.

Suzanne's options

Suzanne has Ivy League written all over her and would have an excellent chance for admission at each one. But she shouldn't look just at the Ivies. The nation's other top schools, such as Duke University in North Carolina, Johns Hopkins University in Baltimore, Georgetown University in Washington, D.C., and the University of Chicago and Northwestern University in Illinois, are also worth considering. But if she wants to stay close to home and attend a top school that will help her reach Harvard Law, a good choice would be Stanford University.

Marshall

Marshall attends a small high school with fewer than 200 students in rural Oklahoma. Although his hometown is quite small, many of the people in the area—including his parents—operate large ranches and agribusinesses and are quite well off. For this reason, the school district has a healthy budget, and Marshall's high school has a surprising number of resources for one its size. More than 60 percent of its graduates go on to college.

Marshall has flourished in this environment. He has a 3.2 GPA and SAT scores of 540 in verbal and 620 in math. Although he hasn't decided on a career, he has a strong interest in biology and the sciences and thinks he might like to pursue a major in a related area. There's also a good chance he'll return home to help run his family's cotton farming and cattle operation, so he'd like to take business courses as well.

Marshall is a successful athlete. He is the star quarterback on his school's six-man football team, a brand of football unique to the small towns of the rural West, and a wrestler. He also competes in rodeos. He has worked as a volunteer in the school library and is the treasurer of the student council.

Having grown up in a rural area and attended a school with so few students, he's anxious to go to a large school that will provide him with a wide range of options and help him broaden his horizons. But he also prefers to stay in the Southwest and remain reasonably close to home. His parents are comfortable financially, so costs are not an issue.

Marshall's options.

Because he wants to stay in the Southwest but study at a large school with diverse offerings, Marshall would probably be happiest at one of the region's state universities. As an Oklahoma resident, two of his best bets would be Oklahoma State and the University of Oklahoma because of the in-state tuition advantages they offer. Other possibilities are the University of Texas, the University of Colorado, Arizona State, and the University of Missouri.

Anna

Anna is a student at a high school in a midsized town in upstate New York. Her parents are divorced, and she has lived with her mother and younger brother since she was eight. Her father lives in the Midwest and, although he's fairly diligent about child support, rarely has contact with the family.

Although Anna has a sharp mind, her family structure has had a negative effect on her school performance. Because her mother works long and irregular hours as a nurse, Anna has shouldered many of the child care duties for her brother almost since the day her parents separated. She is also responsible for a lot of the housework and cooking. This has both distracted her from her schoolwork and prevented her from participating in many extracurricular activities. Quiet and shy, she's almost a nonentity at school. She has few friends and is usually overlooked by her teachers.

Anna wants to attend college and thinks she might like to go into nursing like her mother. She has maintained a C average and her SAT scores are 520 in math and 510 in verbal. However, her mother has little money saved, and she can't count on her father for financial assistance, so paying the bills will be difficult.

Anna's options.

Anna's story is typical of many kids with divorced parents in the United States. For a number of reasons, the most obvious of which is financial, students whose parents have split up are 30 percent less likely to attend college than those whose parents are together. And because of the upheaval they've experienced in their family lives, many of those who do go on to college need help developing good study skills.

Still, Anna has many options open to her. First of all, she's a prime candidate for financial aid, so paying the bills should be within reach. Because of her academic and social history, she'd be better off looking at small schools where she can get any remedial help she might need rather than large universities where she might fall between the cracks. Living in New York State, she can pick from many of the small, relatively inexpensive state colleges that are part of the State University system.

Another excellent strategy would be to enroll in a local community college. There she can hone her academic skills and also enroll in introductory nursing courses to get an idea if she'd like to pursue it as a career. Later, if she chooses, she can transfer to a four-year college or enroll in a nursing program.

Daniel

Daniel is an only child who comes from a family of academics. His parents both teach at an Ivy League university, and his paternal grandparents were also academics. Education is given the highest priority in his family, and Daniel has been raised with the clear expectation that he will pursue advanced degrees in whatever field he chooses. He also knows that following his parents into higher education would make them both very happy. At the moment, however, Daniel is very interested in writing and has his heart set on becoming a novelist or screenwriter.

Daniel attends the public high school in his town and has also taken courses at the university where his parents teach. During his sophomore year, he lived in Italy while his parents were there on sabbatical, and he became quite fluent in Italian. He has lived up to their expectations, maintaining an A average while taking every AP course that's offered. His SAT scores are also good—710 in math and 680 in verbal.

Despite the pressure he has been under to perform academically, Daniel has managed to achieve success in other areas as well. He's an accomplished actor with several major roles in school productions, one of which he wrote, and with a local theater group to his credit. He's been active in school activities and has volunteered with several social service organizations. He also excels in soccer and was named to the all-star team in his league. He would like to play in college.

Daniel's parents want him to attend an Ivy League school. They realize, however, that he needs to get away from home and haven't pressured him to enroll where they teach, even though his tuition would be free. Regardless of where he chooses to go, years of saving and their $150,000 joint annual income will cover the expenses.

Daniel's not so sure about the Ivy League, however. He's a bit weary of high-stress academics and thinks he might be happier at a school where the pressure is a bit less intense. He figures he'll hit the Ivy League for graduate school. In the meantime, he wants to go to a school where he can pursue his interest in writing. He prefers a small- to medium-sized college where he can get to know his professors. He also wants to be near either New York City or Los Angeles.

Daniel's options.

From a purely economic point of view, Daniel's best bet would be to apply to his parents' university. As a faculty brat with excellent grades, he's a shoo-in for admission. And the fact that his parents would only have to pay for fees and room and board makes it a great deal financially.

But the school is much larger than Daniel is looking for, and he really wants to get away from his hometown. He needs a smaller school with a quality humanities program. If he wants to stay in the East, good bets would be Williams College in Massachusetts; Swarthmore College in Pennsylvania; Barnard College in New York City; or Vassar College in Poughkeepsie, New York. If he looks west, he should consider California's Pepperdine University, the University of San Francisco, or Stanford University.

Jess

Jess attends a public high school in a college community in the Northwest. She's a free spirit with a sharp intellect and a maturity beyond her years. She has a keen interest in political and environmental issues and has been active with local environmental groups. Her interest in volunteering comes from her parents, both of whom are active in a wide variety of organizations. Her mother is a professor and her father is director of a privately funded foundation that provides financial support for research on social issues.

Jess has a solid academic record. She's a B+ student with SAT scores of 650 in math and 610 in verbal. She has taken a variety of honors courses and spent a summer working and studying in England through a program run by the local college. She has a number of eclectic interests, including Tae Kwon Do, in which she earned a black belt at the age of 14, and which she teaches at a local club. She plays the piano and has studied both jazz and classical music. She's also a member of a rock-climbing club.

Jess has no firm career goals at this point, but she knows she wants to attend a school that will let her explore her various interests and have close interaction with the faculty. The last thing she wants is a "sheepskin factory," as she put it. She's more concerned with being in an intellectual environment than a social environment. She also would prefer to be in a small- to medium-sized town rather than a city.

Jess's parents have an income of around $110,000. She has an older sister who's a senior in college and a brother who's a high school freshman, so she will be applying for financial aid.

Jess's options.

A student like Jess would be wise to look at liberal arts colleges with reputations for superb student/faculty dynamics, political and social activism, and intense intellectual exploration. A number of schools around the country are known for these qualities. They include Bowdoin College in Maine, Oberlin College in Ohio, Reed College in Oregon, Haverford College in Pennsylvania, and Hamilton College in New York.

Nick

Nick is a junior in a private boarding school in Connecticut. He's a classic underachiever with SATs of 640 in math and 580 in verbal but a GPA of only 2.45. He has excelled in areas that interest him, such as art and music, but has done less well in core curriculum subjects like history and biology. He hasn't been too involved in extracurricular activities in his school, but he is an accomplished musician who plays in a band, and he's a defenseman for his school's ice hockey team. Although his grades have been uneven, his SAT scores and the fact that he shines in areas that he loves indicate that he has the ability to do extremely well when he applies himself.

Nick wants to stay in the Northeast and feels he would be comfortable at a smaller school with an atmosphere similar to that of the private school he attends. But he'd also like to be close to a city. He's completely undecided about career plans and would like to spend a year or two taking a variety of courses. He does not want an academic pressure cooker.

Nick's father is an investment banker, and his mother has an antiques business. With a combined annual income of $375,000, paying for Nick's college education will not be a problem for them.

Nick's options.

Nick would be happiest at a small school that will allow him the freedom to explore his different interests for a while. Since he wants to stay in the Northeast and be near a city, he should look at schools near New York, Philadelphia, and Boston. His candidates might include Marist College in Poughkeepsie, New York; Drew University in New Jersey; St. Joseph's University outside Philadelphia; and Wheaton College and Hampshire College in Massachusetts.

Kendra

Kendra attends a large public high school in Philadelphia. She's enrolled in a specialized curriculum for promising students who come from disadvantaged backgrounds. Both her parents have passed away, and she and her two older sisters live with their maternal grandmother.

Kendra's curriculum emphasizes math and the sciences and has awakened in her a keen interest in biology and genetics. She wants to pursue biology as a major in college and is even giving some thought to going on to medical school. Her GPA is 3.78 and her SAT scores are 690 in math and 640 in verbal. She's president of the student government, volunteers in the school library, and is a member of the debate and tennis teams. She also volunteers at a local hospital.

There is no money in Kendra's family for college, so she will rely entirely on scholarships, grants, and loans. Her older sister attends college in Maryland on a scholarship, and her other sister is going to school part-time at a college in Philadelphia and working at a part-time job. Kendra has been told by her guidance counselor that with her academic record and test scores, she has an excellent chance of receiving a full scholarship to any number of schools. In fact, she has already received literature, unsolicited, from several colleges and universities.

Kendra's options.

Kendra is the type of student that many colleges would love to have. Her potential to excel is clear, as is her desire to work hard. Plus, as a minority and a female who's interested in the sciences, she fits neatly into two gaps that many schools are anxious to fill. Scholarships should not be a problem.

If Kendra wants to stay close to home and receive an excellent education, the University of Pennsylvania is just a few miles away. If she'd like a change of scene, another excellent Ivy League candidate is Cornell University in upstate New York. Other good options include Emory University in Atlanta, George Washington University in Washington, D.C., the University of Delaware, and Johns Hopkins University in Baltimore.

As you can see from the stories of these eight students, there are endless considerations to be made when deciding which college or university is right for you. The key is to start early and do as much research as possible. Be honest in your evaluations of your talents, goals, and desires, and look hard for schools that will provide the best match. And don't worry. There are plenty out there to pick from. If you conduct your search correctly, you won't be disappointed.

FOR MORE INFORMATION

Here are some books and other publications that will come in handy during the college selection process.

- *U.S. News and World Report's Guide to America's Best Colleges,* U.S. News and World Report, Washington, D.C. Published annually.
- *Peterson's Guide to Four-Year Colleges,* Peterson's Guides, Princeton, New Jersey. Published annually.
- *The College Handbook,* College Entrance Examination Board, New York. Published annually.
- *America's Black Colleges* by J. Wilson Bowman, Sandcastle Publishing, Pasadena, Calif. 1992.
- *Opening College Doors—How to Make the Admissions Process Work for You* by Pat Ordovensky and Robert Thornton, Harper Collins, New York. 1992.

- *How to Get an Ivy League Education at a State University* by Martin Nemko, Avon Books, New York. 1988.
- *Looking Beyond the Ivy League* by Loren Pope, Penguin Books, New York. 1990.
- *Handbook for College Admissions* by Thomas C. Hayden, Peterson's Guides, Princeton, N.J. 1989.
- *Women's Colleges* by Joanne Adler and Jennifer Adler Friedman, Arco, New York. 1994.

WHAT'S NEXT?

The rest of this book looks at the really hard part of going to college—paying the bills. For a lucky few, those with enormous incomes or family money, paying for college won't be a problem. But for the rest of us it will be a struggle that combines our own financial resources, loans, scholarships, grants, and whatever else we can beg, borrow, or steal.

The next section of this book looks at investing for college. We'll examine both conservative approaches and high-risk strategies. Not everyone has the same amount of time to get ready, so we'll also look at several investment strategies based on the number of years until your child enters college.

PAYING THE BILLS

PART 1
YOUR CONTRIBUTION

Twenty or thirty years ago, you probably never would have thought that when it became your turn to put children through college it would be this expensive. Back when you were in school, the cost of college had your parents pinching their pennies and thinking twice about that new refrigerator or that weekend out of town. For you, it's the equivalent of buying a second home.

WILL YOU BE READY?

It depends to a large degree on your socioeconomic status. If you're wealthy, you obviously won't have a problem. The cash flow will be there. If you're poor, you probably won't have too much of a problem, either. Colleges are clamoring for talented students from underprivileged backgrounds, and they toss scholarships at them by the handful.

But if you're a member of the middle class, you're in trouble. Yours is the socioeconomic group that has really suffered from the huge escalation in the price of a college education. While wealthy families can afford to pay their own way, and poor families are having their way paid for them, middle-class families are finding themselves priced out of the market.

Over the last 15 years, as college costs have skyrocketed, the middle class has had to contend with a shifting economy that for many has resulted in downward economic mobility and sporadic unemployment. At the same time, they've had to continue to pay for significant portions of their children's college expenses, and they're finding it harder and harder to do. There is real concern that higher education is gradually becoming unattainable to this huge segment of the population. That's a lot of talent down the drain, raising serious concerns about the future of the nation.

A study by the National Institute of Independent Colleges and Universities illustrates just how daunting some parents see the prospect of sending their kids to college. While a third of the parents in the study said they would like to send their children to a private college, fewer than half of those expected to be able to afford it. The study also revealed some other interesting facts.

- 62 percent of parents expected to use personal savings for college, but only 50 percent reported saving on a regular basis.
- 23 percent said they were unable to save and didn't expect to be able to start in the immediate future.
- Of those who were able to save, the average amount put aside was just over $500 a year.
- Nearly 40 percent expected their children to receive scholarships or some other form of financial assistance.
- A third expected to take out loans to pay for college.
- 31 percent expected to pay with money earned while their children are enrolled in college.
- 40 percent expected their children to contribute to the costs of college.
- Only a quarter of parents expected to use state and federal programs as potential sources of funding.
- Most favored a tax incentive plan that would give them a tax credit for money put aside for college.

So if you're a member of that large group of Americans who live from paycheck to paycheck, who aren't poor but for whom luxuries are rare, the challenge of paying for college is enormous. You need to plan very carefully and begin saving as soon as possible.

IT'S TIME TO START INVESTING

For any investor, no matter the goal, the bottom line is simple. You need to start socking away as much as possible in investments that provide the greatest return possible.

Some people have a real aversion to dealing with money. To them, investing is a very daunting concept. If you're one of these people, I'll point out that I've seen many people like you who, once they get involved and begin to educate themselves, become absolute financial addicts. It becomes a big game. In fact, I have friends I consider to be more knowledgeable about investing than some of the stockbrokers I know. Once you get started, you may become like them, with your nose buried in the *Wall Street Journal* every morning.

This brings up a good point. You can—and should—turn to professionals for help (we'll discuss the role of financial planners later in this chapter), but this is too important an issue to leave solely to other people. You really have a responsibility to educate yourself. Read about investment strategies. Pick up financial publications like the *Wall Street Journal* and *Barron's* and *Money* magazine. If you're proactive in your approach to investing, you'll be able to have much more constructive conversations with financial advisers and stockbrokers. You'll also feel a lot more confident in your investment decisions.

HOW MUCH WILL YOU NEED?

It depends on the age of your child. In 1996–97, the average cost for four years at a private college or university was approximately $92,000. The average for public colleges and universities was about $40,000. For each year until your child will be entering college, you can count on those numbers increasing by 5 to 6 percent or more.

The following chart illustrates a 5.5 percent annual increase in college costs. (With any luck, actual increases will be less. However, they also could be higher.) The chart shows how much you can expect to pay when your child reaches college. Obviously, the older your child, the less you'll pay. But if you have an infant staring expectantly up at you from the crib, the news is shocking. You can figure on shelling out more than $100,000 for a public university and more than $240,000 for a private university.

There is some good news however. Most of you won't need to raise the complete cost of your child's education. The average student today pays about 60 percent of college costs with savings and unsubsidized loans. The rest is covered by grants, scholarships, and subsidized loans.

Still, it's important to remember that having a healthy chunk of money set aside will increase your child's options when it comes time to apply to colleges. Colleges are more than willing to chip in to help you put together a financial package that will cover your costs. In fact, they're remarkably generous. But they do expect you to carry your share of the load. So your ability to pay is a deciding factor in opening a lot of doors.

THE AVERAGE COST OF A FOUR-YEAR COLLEGE EDUCATION

Child's age in 1998	*Public college*	*Private college*
18	$40,000	$92,000
17	$42,200	$97,060
16	$44,520	$102,400
15	$46,970	$108,030
14	$49,550	$113,970
13	$52,280	$120,240
12	$55,150	$126,850
11	$58,190	$133,830
10	$61,390	$141,190
9	$64,760	$148,960
8	$68,330	$157,150
7	$72,080	$165,800
6	$76,050	$174,910
5	$80,230	$184,540
4	$84,640	$194,680
3	$89,300	$205,390
2	$94,210	$216,690
1	$99,390	$228,600
Newborn	$104,860	$241,180

WHEN SHOULD YOU START SAVING?

Have you ever seen the T-shirts printed with a picture of an alarmed 30-something-ish career woman with her hand on her forehead saying, "Oh, no! I forgot to have children!" There should be a similar shirt for procrastinating parents—"Oh, no! I forgot to save for college!"

Obviously, the more time you have to save, the easier it will be to reach your goal. So saving for college should start the day a child is born. However, that rarely happens. Most of us think to ourselves, "It's 18 years away. I have plenty of time." But all too often 18 years suddenly becomes 10 years or 8 years or 4 years. We've been running around enjoying nice vacations, furnishing the house, buying new cars, and going out to dinner far more often than we should. Then one day we wake up and realize we have to come up with a lot of money in a very short period of time. It's not that we haven't thought about it. We just never managed to get organized.

Just remember it's never too late to start. Even if your child is entering high school, you still have four years until you write your first tuition check. You're not going to save everything you'll need between now and then, but you can at least make a dent in it.

CREATE A BUDGET

Saving and investing require discipline. You'll be diverting a significant amount of money into your college fund, so your cash flow is going to be diminished. The large purchases you used to make on a whim will now require some planning. Some luxuries may be out of the question altogether. If you've always pretty much bought whatever you wanted, having less disposable income will take some getting used to

The best way to get your finances under control is to create a monthly budget. It's the only way to guarantee that the money will be put aside. First, write down all your fixed expenses like your mortgage, car loans, property taxes, and insurance premiums. Then take a look at the expenses you have some control over, such as the phone bill, the cable television bill, and the utility bill. Look back at your payments for the previous year and write down a reasonable monthly amount to budget for each one.

That still leaves food, clothing, gasoline, medical expenses, entertainment, and any other expenses you may have. Budget money for each one. Whatever is left over can be invested. If it's less than you had hoped, you'll need to ask yourself the next question.

IS IT TIME FOR A LIFESTYLE CHANGE?

Saving for college means making sacrifices. If you and your spouse have been enjoying the trappings of the two-income, childless lifestyle, kiss it good-by. Forget the BMW, the ski vacations to Colorado, the fancy restaurants, the clothes, the health club. You're no longer a Yuppie. You've become a PUPPY—a Parent Under Pressure. Welcome to the club.

When they stop and take a really hard look at their spending habits, most people discover they are able to cut back significantly. Some go from being a two-car family to being a one-car family. Buying at retail becomes a mortal sin. They start to clip coupons and pay attention to the number of long-distance phone calls they make. They cut down on trips to the movies. Dinner out becomes a trip to the pizza parlor around the corner, rather than to the four-star French restaurant downtown. Some even decide they can be just as happy in a less expensive house with a cheaper mortgage.

Another good bit of advice is to hide your credit cards. Unless you use them as they are intended to be used—to avoid using cash or checks to make purchases—and pay your balance off every month, they can become a real threat to your ability to save. It's extremely easy to build up credit card debt, and at 17 to 20 percent interest, the monthly payments can become overwhelming.

SHOULD YOU CONSULT A FINANCIAL PLANNER?

Yes, and do it before you start your savings plan. If you've always thought financial planners were only for wealthy people, you're wrong. In addition to advising you on investments, a good financial planner can help you set up a budget to control your spending and make sure you have the proper insurance. Almost all financial services companies have developed programs specifically for families who are saving for college. Many banks and insurance companies offer them, too.

Having said all that, I'll also point out that many financial planners are idiots, so you'll need to be very careful in your selection. In chapter 3 we'll look at some of the problems.

It's also important to involve your whole family in the plan. Let your kids know what you're doing and explain why. If there are going to be any major changes in lifestyle, they need to understand the reason. Most kids don't have a clue about finances and how their parents manage the family money. By making them a part of the process, you'll be teaching them lessons in fiscal responsibility that will hopefully carry over to their own adult lives.

You also should talk to your insurance agent and your attorney. You need to make sure your insurance policies and your will are set up to provide the money for college if you should pass away. (We'll look at this issue in greater detail later in the book.)

THE CLOCK IS TICKING

So what's the big deal? All you have to do is save for something whose cost is increasing at three times the rate of inflation with a salary that's probably just managing to keep pace with inflation. Geez, you'd think you had a problem or something.

Actually, the challenge before you is enormous. But don't panic. With a sound investment strategy, you can build a college nest egg that, combined with assistance from your child's college, will pay the bills. The next few chapters will help you get your nest egg rolling.

We'll start with the investments traditionally used to save for college, from savings accounts and certificates of deposit to stocks and bonds to mutual funds. You may even be able to borrow against a retirement fund or an insurance policy. We'll examine your investment options and compare levels of risk. Depending on your needs, you'll find that some or all of them are worth using.

3

A LOOK AT INVESTING BASICS

There's an old saying on Wall Street that speaks volumes about how people should approach the art of investing: "Bears make money. Bulls make money. Pigs get slaughtered."

In other words, investing is a long-term endeavor in which patience is rewarded. In fact, time is as much a factor in investment success as anything else. If you want to make money overnight, go to Atlantic City or Las Vegas. Just remember that most people in those towns end up as bacon.

To illustrate the point, consider this: If you put just $10 aside every week from the time your child is born, and the money appreciates at 8 percent, on his or her 18th birthday your child will have $20,993. If you put away $15 a week, the amount will be $48,196. So by setting aside an amount of money that to most families is insignificant, and letting time work its magic, you can create a nest egg that will go a long way toward meeting college expenses. This is why starting early is so critical. The longer you can hold on to an investment, the better your chances of enjoying a profit.

A FEW WORDS ABOUT RISK

If you play golf, you're familiar with the concept of risk versus reward. When you're faced with a dogleg tee shot you have two choices: you can play it safe and hit the ball straight to the corner and leave yourself a mid- to long-iron approach to the green, or you can try to crank it over the trees at the corner and leave yourself a little wedge shot into the green. The high-risk shot provides the higher reward.

Risk is an inherent element of investing and, as in golf, is present in direct correlation to potential return. For example, the safest and most conservative investments, such as savings accounts and certificates of deposit, are insured and risk-free. But they also have quite low rates of return. You can put your money in a savings account or buy a CD secure in the knowledge that it's safely snuggled away with a large, federally insured institution. The downside is that it's earning interest at a relatively snail-like pace.

The other side of the coin is to throw caution to the wind and go to Atlantic City or Las Vegas for the big score. Take your money to a casino, find a roulette wheel, and bet it all on red. It's an extremely short-term investment (about 10 seconds) with about as high a risk/return ratio as you can ask for. If the ball lands on red, you've doubled your money. If it lands on black, you're slaughtered.

Of course, only an idiot would actually do such a thing (I know—I'm acquainted with some of these idiots personally). You'll be putting your money in investments that are quite conservative by casino standards. Still, there's a fairly wide range of risk within the overall spectrum of investment choices. We'll consider risk as we examine different investments you might use to build your child's college nest egg.

A FEW WORDS ABOUT BROKERS AND FINANCIAL PLANNERS

When you begin to invest money, you're going to get involved with investment brokers and financial planners. A broker acts as the agent between the buyer and the seller of a security. In exchange for this service he charges a fee, called a commission. A financial planner provides consultation and advice for a flat fee. Some have the impressive title ''certified financial planner'' and prominently include the CFP on their business cards and advertising. My advice? Don't be impressed.

Brokers usually also act as financial planners. They recommend certain securities based on the needs of each client. Full-service brokers recommend and sell stocks, bonds, mutual funds, investment certificates, annuities, and most other investment vehicles. Many work for big firms like Merrill Lynch and Kidder Peabody. Others work for tiny firms most people have never heard of.

Many people prefer to work with just one broker. This is fine as long as the broker is knowledgeable in the securities you're interested in. Some brokers specialize in bonds or mutual funds but only have a rudimentary knowledge of other types of investments. But if you plan to be more diverse in your investing, having several experts on your side is probably the more prudent approach.

Most brokers are honest, well-trained individuals who work hard on behalf of their clients and do their best to help them make money. But there are also brokers who are only interested in getting into your wallet by selling you whatever security they can get you to buy. Your long-term financial health is not on their agenda. Here's a personal story that illustrates the types of scams some people will pull to get your business.

My Life as a Pigeon

Over the last couple of years I've received the same phone call from three different gentlemen.

''Mr. Powers, this is (so-and-so) from (so-and-so) investment company,'' they begin. ''You probably remember we spoke about six months ago about (this-or-that) security. I sent you some literature and I'm calling back to see what you thought about the investment.''

Well, the first time this happened, I was polite, even though I didn't remember having the conversation or getting the literature. I confessed to my failing memory and we talked for a minute or two. Then he asked me for my address.

BINGO! The lightbulb went off.

''Wait a minute,'' I said. ''I thought you just said you sent me some literature. How did you do that if you don't have my address?''

At this point he got a little flustered. I wrapped up the conversation quickly, irritated but remaining polite.

The second time it happened, I let the guy get through his spiel, then told him I wasn't interested and hung up.

But the third time it happened, I lost it. Before the weasel got halfway through his story, I interrupted him.

"Hold it right there," I yelled. "You're full of #!@*#! We've never spoken before and you know it. Why don't you get a real job?! Don't ever bother me again!"

As you might guess, investors have been complaining about brokers for years. Some of their complaints are valid; there are lots of jerks like the three idiots who called me with the pathetic little scam I just described. Other complaints are just sour grapes. Investing is always a gamble, and people sometimes do lose money, no matter how talented their broker may be.

The Conflict of Interest Problem

A big part of the problem is that brokers are working for themselves, for their employers, and for their clients, and their clients' interests might not always come first. While you're trying to save to put your kid through college, your broker may be trying to earn money to put his kid through college, too. This can sometimes lead to conflict between broker and client.

This is because brokers work on commission. They only make money when you buy or sell a security. And it doesn't matter whether you make money or not. If a broker recommends a stock and you decide to buy it, he makes a commission on the sale. If the stock goes down in value and you sell it, he makes a commission again on that transaction. So while you've lost money on your little venture, he's made a tidy profit even though he gave you lousy advice. This has led many people to suggest that brokers should only make commissions when they steer you to investments that make a profit. (Of course, this will never happen.)

Searching for Good Financial Planners

When you begin to look for a financial planner, ask around for some recommendations. The best sources of information are people who are experienced investors. I know a guy who won $8.4 million in the New York State Lottery a few years ago. He was a meat cutter in a grocery store, and his wife worked in the back office in a Kmart. I asked him if there was a downside to their good fortune.

"The biggest problem was we didn't know anything about investing," he said. "We had always lived from paycheck to paycheck and had a savings account, but that was about it. So I started talking to doctors and lawyers I knew, figuring they had money to invest. They introduced us to some people who have done a good job helping us manage the money.''

When you're talking to financial planners, explain what your goals are and how long you have to reach them. Ask them how much experience they have in helping people save for college. You might want to find out if they have children approximately the same age as yours. If they do, it more than likely means they're already devising their own investment strategy to pay for college. Here are some other questions that will need answering.

How do they earn their income?

If it's solely from fees, you're generally safe. But if a portion of their income comes from commissions on the sale of investment products, the person may be more interested in making sure you buy something than in helping you plan for your needs.

What's their hourly fee?

This may seem like a no-brainer, but you'd be amazed at how many people either fail to ask beforehand or are just too intimidated to ask. Some financial planners charge as little as $50 an hour, and some charge several hundred dollars an hour. Generally speaking, though, you should be able to find good people for about $100 an hour.

What are their qualifications?

How long have they been in the financial planning field? What did they do before that? What financial planning courses have they taken? All these questions will help you get some idea of how qualified they really are.

As I mentioned earlier, some financial planners will have earned the title ''certified financial planner'' and will wave their CFP flag as evidence of their competence. Don't get too excited. Anyone can become a certified financial planner by taking a mail order home study course and passing an easy test administered by the College for Financial Planning.

Do they offer other services such as tax services or legal services?

If they do, beware. You want an expert, and these fields are too complex for a person to be competent in each. If you want tax advice, see a tax specialist. If you want legal advice, see a lawyer.

Do they carry liability insurance?

Liability insurance? A financial planner? You bet. Financial planners can make mistakes that cost their clients a great deal of money. Sometimes they're liable for their errors. If they are, and it's your money that's been lost, the fact that they have liability insurance will guarantee that you'll get your investment back. Remember, investing wisely means minimizing risk. This is one way to do just that.

Have they worked with other clients whose primary investment goal was to save for college, or are they saving for their own children's education?

Ask the planner's clients how the planner's advice worked out. Ask if they enjoyed working with the planner. The answers will help you get an idea of the planner's strengths and weaknesses.

You Need to Educate Yourself

Once you find a good broker or financial planner, don't accept everything he or she says as gospel. As I mentioned earlier, it's extremely important to educate yourself. You need to be proactive in your approach to investing, and you need to be able to discuss various options with your broker and understand the investment decisions that are made.

Discount Brokers

Discount brokers charge a reduced commission for their services. They do this because they don't try to sell people investments; they just execute trades. They're popular with people who prefer to do their own market research and make their own investment decisions. If you get to the point where you're comfortable calling your own shots, use a discount broker. There's no reason to pay for a service you don't need. On the next page is a list of some of the biggest.

- Accutrade (800-228-3011)
- Ceres Securities (800-669-3900)
- Charles Schwab & Co. (800-435-4000)
- E*Trade (800-786-2575)
- Fidelity Brokerage (800-544-8666)
- Freedom Investments (800-944-4033)
- Kennedy Cabot (800-252-0090)
- Jack White (800-233-3411)
- Muriel Siebert (800-872-0444)
- National Discount Brokers (800-417-7423)
- Quick & Reilly (800-221-5220)
- Vanguard Discount Brokerage (800-992-8327)
- Waterhouse Securities (800-934-4410)

Investment Clubs

If you like the idea of making your own decisions and don't mind the input of other investors, putting some money into an investment club might appeal to you. These are groups of people who pool their money to buy not just stocks but other securities as well. Some of them have turned in fantastic performances over the years.

Investment clubs have regular meetings, where members discuss and vote on proposed investments. Members contribute an agreed upon amount each month—sometimes as little as $10 or $20—to put toward investments and cover the cost of brokers' commissions. One of the benefits of these clubs is the chance to learn how other people approach investing. You may learn a few tricks you can apply to your private accounts.

GETTING STARTED—SOME TRADITIONAL INVESTING INSTRUMENTS

As a novice investor, you'll quickly learn there are many investments to pick from. We'll begin with the most popular, most common, and safest. Later in the book we'll look at some of the more unusual options, including, oddly enough, investments called "options."

Savings Accounts

Savings accounts are the simplest method for putting money aside. You open an account with a bank and are issued a passbook. Every transaction in the account—deposits, withdrawals, and interest earned—is recorded in the passbook. You can deposit or withdraw as much money as you wish anytime you wish. Interest rates fluctuate, and the money in the account is insured by the United States government through the Federal Deposit Insurance Corporation (FDIC).

Savings accounts are as safe as mother's milk. But because they're risk free, their interest rates are quite low. Still, if you're starting to put money aside while your children are young, putting a few dollars in a passbook account is a great way to teach them the basics of investing. Let them control the account and make the deposits, and explain to them how interest works.

Certificates of Deposit

Certificates of deposit (CDs) are offered by banks. They pay a guaranteed rate of interest over a specified length of time. Some CDs are offered for three- or six-month periods. Others are for a year or more. When the time period is up, you can either take the money out or reinvest it, or "roll it over," into another CD. In fact, if you don't redeem a CD within 10 days of maturity, the bank will automatically roll it over. You can redeem CDs before they mature, but you will pay a penalty. The FDIC insures certificates of deposit up to $100,000 in insured institutions.

As we'll see later in this chapter, certificates of deposit are much like zero-coupon bonds. For example, when you put $1,000 in a 12-month CD, you're really lending the bank your money for a year. In return, the bank promises to pay you back your $1,000 plus an agreed upon rate of interest. But rather than receiving interest payments weekly or monthly, you get it in a lump sum at the end of the 12 months, along with your $1,000. If the interest rate for the CD was 5 percent, you would receive $1,050.

During the 12 months the bank has your $1,000, it's making money by pooling it with other CDs to make car loans, mortgage loans, or business loans at much higher interest rates than it's paying you. The difference between what the bank charges its loan customers and what it pays you in interest is the bank's profit.

Although certificates of deposit don't earn as much interest as many other investments, they're very popular with small investors. They can be purchased in small amounts, they're completely risk-free, and they're easy to buy (you can even buy them through the mail). CDS also are very high profile, and banks advertise them heavily.

But as you compare CDs to other investments reviewed later in this book, you'll learn they're not all that great a deal. Not only do they pay less interest but you also have to pay state and local taxes on the interest they do pay. Still, they do function as good short-term "parking" spots for your money while you investigate other options.

Investment Certificates

Investment certificates are just like certificates of deposit. But instead of being issued by banks and protected by the FDIC, they're issued by investment firms and are backed by the reserves of the issuing firms. Like CDs, they come in a variety of denominations and have varying lengths of maturity.

FOR MORE INFORMATION

In the next few chapters, I'll be recommending books that deal exclusively with different types of investments. But for a good overall look at managing your money and the challenges of investing, here are a few recommendations.

- *Personal Finance for Dummies,* 2nd Ed. by Eric Tyson, IDG Books Worldwide, San Mateo, California, 1996.
- *The Wall Street Journal Guide to Money and Investing* by Kenneth M. Morris and Alan M. Siegel, Lightbulb Press, New York, 1996.
- *The Only Investment Guide You'll Ever Need* by Andrew Tobias, Harcourt Brace & Company, New York, 1996.

WHAT'S NEXT?

Savings accounts and certificates of deposit are certainly safe investments, but they're not going to earn you very much money. They're not going to make your life very exciting, either.

To earn more money and generate a little excitement, you need to learn about and invest in some of the securities that really drive Wall Street. We'll begin with the most basic—stocks. They're fun to follow and, if chosen carefully, can earn you a lot of money. We'll look at stocks in chapter 4.

4

STOCKS—THE INVESTOR AS OWNER

Stocks are a traditional favorite of investors. When you buy a share of stock in a company, you become a part owner of the company. You join the thousands, or even millions, of other people who also own stock in the company. The more shares you own, the bigger your chunk of the corporate pie.

Stocks can be a nerve-racking way to put your money to work, but history shows they do pay off. Over the years, the stock market has outperformed every other type of investment.

WHY DO COMPANIES ISSUE STOCK?

It's very simple—to raise cash. Most new companies are created with money raised from investors such as venture capitalists. As these companies grow and bring a product or two to the market, they may begin to gather some momentum. But their ability to grow further is frequently hampered by a lack of capital.

This is where stock comes in. To raise the money needed to continue their growth, these companies offer stock to the public—they "go public" with an "initial public offering" (IPO). They work with investment bankers to determine how many shares to offer and how much to charge per share. The investment bank then agrees to "underwrite" the offering. This means the bank buys all the shares and then resells them to the public.

Down the road, if they need to raise even more capital, some companies will sell additional stock through a secondary offering. The problem with this strategy is that it weakens the value of existing shares, a situation that doesn't make shareholders too happy. As an alternative to issuing more stock, most companies will begin to issue bonds, a strategy we'll look at later.

WHO BUYS STOCK?

More than 50 million Americans own stock. The average investor has about a third of his or her total investment portfolio in stocks.

But the biggest buyers of stock are institutional investors—pension funds, mutual funds, insurance companies, universities, and other large organizations. Decisions affecting these huge accounts are made by fund managers, men and women who spend their days buying and selling the securities in the fund to maximize profits. Their holdings are enormous. State pension funds alone have tens of billions of dollars' worth of stock in their coffers, and they trade regularly and in enormous volume. Buying or selling blocks of 50,000 or more shares at a time is a daily event.

WHAT TYPES OF STOCK ARE AVAILABLE?

Almost all stock falls within one of two categories—common and preferred.

Common stocks are the basic ownership shares in a company. They're purchased by a wide variety of individuals and institutions and are continually traded among investors; on a busy day, more than 400 million shares change hands. What was at the time the biggest trading day in history—October 20, 1987, the day after the market crashed and lost 22 percent of its value—saw more than 600 million shares traded as investors struggled to staunch their wounds.

The owners of common stock receive periodic dividends. There are no guarantees on how much a dividend will be; they fluctuate with the company's performance. The stock price also fluctuates with performance. The lucky investor will see his stock steadily increase in value at a rate that outperforms other investments. The unlucky investor will watch his stock become worthless as the company goes down the tubes and eventually out of business. But at least his losses will stop there. Fortunately, shareholders are not responsible for a company's debts.

Preferred stocks are also ownership shares that are traded by investors. But they differ from common stock in several important ways. One, the dividend is guaranteed and is paid before the dividends for common stock are paid. Two, the dividend doesn't change, no matter how poorly—or wonderfully—the company performs. And three, the value of preferred stock increases more slowly than the value of common stock does.

ARE STOCKS HIGH-RISK INVESTMENTS?

They can be. It depends on the financial condition of the company whose stock you buy. Some stocks, such as those of the 30 companies that make up the Dow Jones Industrial Average, are considered "blue chips." They're older, established companies like DuPont, General Motors, and IBM, whose performances, although certainly vulnerable to peaks and valleys, generally can be counted on for steady growth. This, in turn, means healthy dividends and a steady increase in the price of their stock Risk is minimal.

At the other end of the spectrum are exciting young companies competing in boom industries like computers and biotechnology. Investments in these companies offer the potential for great profit. They also carry a larger degree of risk. There are many such companies out there, and the stock of many of them will outperform much of the rest of the market. Investors who choose wisely make a lot of money. (Don't you wish you'd gotten into Microsoft on the ground floor?) Those who don't sometimes lose their shirts.

The value of some stocks is very closely tied to the overall condition of the economy. In times of economic downturn, their values fall. When the economy begins an upswing, their prices recover. Hotel stocks, for instance, usually follow this pattern. This is because when the economy is poor, people cut down on travel and vacations.

HOW DO YOU BUY AND SELL STOCK?

It's easy. Just call your broker. Let's say you decide to buy 100 shares of the XYZ Corporation. Your broker sends the buy order from his office to a floor broker (usually from the same company) on the stock exchange where XYZ stock is traded. The floor broker purchases the 100 shares and sends a confirmation to your broker, including the number of shares bought and the price per share. You give your broker a check for the price of the stock and his commission. Then you spend every morning you own the stock anxiously checking its price in the stock listings in the newspaper.

Stocks are usually bought and sold in blocks of 100 shares called "round lots." However, you can buy or sell any number you wish, even just a single share. These are called "odd lots" and usually entail a slightly higher commission by brokers.

Investors can put specific conditions on the purchase of stock. If you want to buy the stock at the current price, you place a "market order." If you think the stock might be going down and you want to wait until it drops three or four points, you place a "limit order." This tells the broker that you'll pay no more than whatever's on the order. If you're lucky, the broker might even be able to buy it for a half a point to a point less. If you're selling a stock whose price has been going up, you can do the reverse and tell the broker not to sell until it reaches a certain price. To protect yourself against losses, you can place a "stop-loss order" that dictates the downside price at which you want to sell stock.

Orders to buy or sell can be "day orders," meaning they need to be executed the day they're given to the broker, or "good-til-canceled" orders (GTCs), which stay active until executed or canceled. A day order that's not executed by the end of the day's trading session is automatically canceled.

HOW ARE STOCK ORDERS EXECUTED?

Stocks are bought and sold on the stock exchanges of six cities in the United States—New York (which has two, the New York Stock Exchange and the American Stock Exchange), Chicago, Philadelphia, Boston, Cincinnati, and Los Angeles.

Most people who have seen one of these trading floors in action find it hard to believe that anyone can do business amidst such frenzied activity. But brokers and traders will tell you that once you get used to it, you don't even notice the commotion. They're able to concentrate and do what they have to do. It's a good thing, because they're the people who ultimately are responsible for buying and selling your stock for you.

When a broker sends an order to the trading floor, the floor broker takes the order to the post where the stock is traded. Trading in each stock is controlled by a "specialist" whose job is to facilitate trades and keep trading orderly. The floor broker announces his intent to the brokers and traders in the crowd, who reply by telling him the prices at which they're willing to either buy (the "bid") or sell (the "ask") the stock. These two prices establish what traders call the "market" for the stock.

For example, suppose XYZ stock has been trading at around $30, and you want to buy your 100 shares at the market price. The floor broker announces to the crowd that he wants to buy 100 shares. If he's good, he'll look at where the stock has been trading and bid a half point or so less than its last sale. The sellers in the crowd will reply by telling him what they're asking for the stock. The conversation will go something like this. (I've included translations.)

Floor Broker: Thirty and a quarter for 100. (I'll pay $30.25 a share for 100 shares.)

Sellers: At three-quarters (We want $30.75 a share.)

Floor Broker (if he feels like bargaining): I'll bid a half. (Okay. In that case I'm willing to pay $30.50 a share.)

At this point the sellers will either agree to his bid of $30.50 or stand firm at their asking price of $30.75. Since it's a market order, the floor broker will pay what they're asking if they don't accept his bid.

If you place a limit order, on the other hand, the interaction will be a bit different. Let's say you think XYZ stock is going to drop, and you want to pay $27 a share for it. You ask the broker to put in a GTC buy order with a $27 a share limit. In this case the conversation is likely to go like this.

Floor Broker (with great modesty, knowing he's going to be roundly ridiculed for his low bid): Twenty-seven for a hundred. (I'll pay $27 a share for 100 shares.)

Sellers (falling all over each other in hysterics): In your dreams, big spender. At thirty and three quarters. (Don't come around here wasting our time with that nonsense. We want $30.75 a share.)

Floor Broker (defensively): Yeah, well, what can I say? The guy's an idiot. (Gee, I'm sorry. It would appear that my client [meaning *you*] may be a bit unrealistic in his expectations.)

At this point, since your bid is so far away from where the stock is trading, the floor broker will give your order to the specialist to hold. The specialist will then execute the trade when (and if) the stock reaches your desired price and charge your floor broker a commission for the service. Specialists keep many such orders on their books. It's one way they make money.

Trading Electronically on the NASDAQ

Investors can also buy and sell stock on a nationwide electronic network run by the National Association of Securities Dealers. Brokers are able to monitor prices from their offices on their computer monitors and make trades over the telephone. With 4,700 companies, the NASDAQ lists more than twice as many stocks as the New York Stock Exchange and more than five times as many as the American Stock Exchange. They range from small emerging firms to giants like Apple and Microsoft.

Over-the-counter Trading

The nation's smallest firms are traded "over-the-counter" (OTC), a term that dates back to when investors would literally buy stock over counters at their brokers' offices. There are 28,000 companies whose stock is traded in this manner. Because of their low prices and light trading activity, information on OTC stocks aren't listed electronically. Instead, brokers receive daily reports called "pink sheets" that help them keep track of prices.

HOW DO YOU EARN MONEY AS A STOCKHOLDER?

The stockholders in a company receive periodic payments called "dividends." The amount of dividend paid per share of outstanding stock is determined by the company's board of directors. There's no universal formula for figuring dividends, but the basic rule of thumb is that the better the company performs, the higher the dividend it pays its stockholders.

There are times, however, when a dividend will be smaller than expected because the board of directors decides the money is needed for something else. Rather than float a bond issue or borrow money, they decide to raise the money by keeping dividends smaller. As a part owner of the company, you're expected to be a good trooper and go along with the idea.

But dividends alone don't make stocks a great investment. The real reason people buy stock is to profit from the increase in the stock's price over time. If you buy a stock at $20 per share and a year later sell it for $40 a share, you've made a 100 percent profit, or $20 a share, on your investment.

At any point in time, the prices of individual stocks are rising and falling at various speeds. Every year, the prices of some stocks go through the roof, doubling or even tripling in value. The prices of others go through the floor, leaking value like water dripping out of a rusty bucket. The vast majority, however, gain and lose value more slowly.

In a boom market like the one that has existed during the '90s—as this book was being written the Dow Jones Industrial Average was leaping from one record high to another—most stocks perform well. In a slow market there are still good performers, but prices in general tend to stagnate. Some stocks lose value, others gain. But regardless of the direction of their prices, movement is very slow.

Historically, the stock market has moved in up (a "bull" market) and down (a "bear" market) cycles, although the overall trend has been an upswing. Unfortunately, the ability to forecast market movement is a rare talent indeed. Some factors—low interest rates, a good money supply, high employment, political stability—are known to encourage investment in stocks. When the opposite is true, markets generally fall. Despite this knowledge, explaining actual market behavior is usually only possible with 20/20 hindsight.

ARE THERE OTHER WAS TO MAKE MONEY WITH STOCKS?

There are several. Here are two of the most common.

Shorting is a strategy used to take advantage of falling stock prices. It's a bit confusing because you're actually selling stock you don't own in the hope of buying it back at a lower price and keeping the difference. It works like this.

You open an account with a broker and then from him borrow and sell stock you think is going to fall in price. Let's say you borrow 100 shares of XYZ and sell it at $30 a share, to collect $3,000. Great deal, huh?

There's just one problem. At some point you have to buy the stock back and repay your broker. People who short stock are gambling that the stock will decrease in value and they can repurchase the shares at a lower price. The difference between the two prices is their profit. In your case, if XYZ stock drops to $27 a share and you buy it back for $2,700, you've made a $300 profit (less the interest and commission charged by your broker). But if the stock goes up to $33 before you buy it back, you'll lose $300.

Obviously, selling short is not for the novice investor. It requires a great deal of knowledge about what makes a stock rise and fall in price. It's also a strategy that needs to be carried out quickly to make a good profit because you're paying interest to the broker on the shares you borrowed. There's also the danger of getting caught in a situation where a stock that's heavily shorted begins to rise in price. The ensuring scramble to sell makes its price rise even more quickly and increases your loss even further.

Warrants are another way to gamble on future prices. A warrant allows you, for a fee, to buy a stock at a certain price within a certain period of time. Investors buy warrants when they think the price of a stock is going to increase. Warrants are listed in the stock tables in the newspapers and are actively traded among investors.

For example, you might buy a warrant for a dollar a share that will allow you to buy XYZ stock at $31 a share at any time within the next five years. Two years later the stock has gone up to $35 a share, and you decide to buy. You save $3 a share on each share you purchase You then can turn around and immediately sell the stock for a $3 a share profit.

CAN YOU BORROW MONEY TO BUY STOCKS?

Yes, but not from a bank. That's too expensive and cuts into your profit. Instead you can borrow it directly from your broker and "leverage" your stock purchase. This is called "buying on margin" and works like this.

Let's say that you've decided to buy 200 shares of XYZ stock at $30 a share but you want to use your own money to buy only 100 shares. You set up a margin account with your broker, sign a margin agreement, and maintain a minimum balance in the account ($2,000 in cash or securities). This allows you to borrow the other

$3,000 you need from the broker. In turn, he charges you interest while the loan is outstanding.

Again, like shorting, this looks like a great deal on the face of it. But it only works if the stock goes up in price. Let's say XYZ stock goes up to $35 a share, and you decide to sell. You'll receive $7,000, pay back your broker the $3,000 you borrowed, and enjoy a tidy $1,000 profit, less interest and commissions. And since you only put up $3,000 of your own money, that's almost a 33 percent return on your investment.

Of course, the downside of buying on margin is obvious. If XYZ stock falls, and you're forced to sell at $25 a share, you lose $1,000. And to add to the pain, you'll still owe the broker his commission and interest. (Notice how the broker always gets paid no matter what happens to you?) You're also vulnerable to what's called a "margin call." This occurs when the value of the stock falls below 75 percent of its original value. To protect himself, the broker will demand that you either put more money in your margin account or sell the stock and pay him back. Either way, it's going to cost you money.

WHAT MAKES A STOCK'S PRICE CHANGE?

The price of a share of stock is governed by that most basic economic concept—supply and demand. When more people want to buy a stock than want to sell the stock, the price goes up. When sellers outnumber buyers, the price goes down.

What makes people want to buy a company's stock? A belief that the company will continue to grow and be profitable. As a part owner of the company, they'll share in the profits through the dividends they receive.

But there's another reason that has more to do with emotion than economics. They buy because they think the stock is going to continue to be in demand by other investors. It's a lot like gambling. If enough other people buy the stock, the price will continue to rise. But if investors suddenly begin to think the stock is overvalued or the company is headed for trouble, the stock price can tumble quickly.

One of the problems with stocks is that, as an investor, you're riding the fortunes of whatever companies you happen to own stock in. If you choose wisely and the companies perform well, you make money. Dividends are healthy and the price of the stock rises. If you're really lucky, the stock might split, and the number of shares you own will double.

But if the companies in which you've invested fall on rough times, the opposite can occur. Dividends shrink, and the price of the stock drops. And companies are vulnerable to all sorts of disasters. Think back to the Texaco racial discrimination suit in 1996. The company was already battling the suit in court when an audiotape turned up that depicted company executives using racial slurs. The entire nation immediately pronounced the company guilty, and Texaco stock went through the floor. If you had all your money invested with the company, you'd have been one unhappy camper.

But it's not just incidents like this that can hurt a company. Some just fall on hard times, revenues fall, and their stock slowly loses value over a period of time. Of course, if you're able to ride out the downturn, you might see the company recover and its stock rebound to the point where you end up making a nice profit. Again, this points out the importance of investing for the long haul.

HOW HIGH CAN THE PRICE OF A SHARE GO?

Theoretically, there's no ceiling on the price of a share of stock. In fact, in small, privately held companies whose stock is controlled by just a few people, a single share of stock can be worth thousands of dollars. It depends on the value of the company and how many shares of stock exist.

In publicly held companies, however, a high stock price can discourage investors. Corporations realize this, so many will execute a ''stock split'' when the price of their stock reaches a certain point. When this happens, a share of stock is divided to create additional shares.

Let's say you own 100 shares of a stock that's worth $80 a share and the company declares a two-for-one split. You'll now own 200 shares, each worth $40. The total value of your holdings is still $8,000, it's just held in more units of stock. Hopefully, after the split, the value of the 200 shares will continue to rise.

Stock splits are not executed solely in ratios of two for one. They can be three for one, three for two, five for one, or any other combination. Whatever the ratio, the result is more stock available for a lower price, and that will stimulate investing.

Sometimes a company will execute what's called a "reverse split," in which ten shares may be turned into five, or four into one. In this case, the company is deliberately increasing the per share price in order to discourage small investors. Its goal may be to reduce the number of investors in the company—a move that reduces paperwork and accounting procedures. It may also be to encourage institutional investors, many of whom won't invest in a stock that's trading below a certain price.

IF YOU OWN PART OF THE COMPANY, DO YOU HAVE ANY SAY IN HOW IT'S RUN?

Yes. As a stockholder, you have the right to vote on decisions affecting the company, including appointments to its board of directors. Decisions determined by a vote of the stockholders are usually made at a company's annual shareholders meeting. Because only a very small percentage of a company's stockholders actually attend these meetings, well in advance of the meeting all the shareholders receive in the mail an absentee ballot or "proxy." You cast your vote on the different proposals and board candidates, sign and date the proxy, and return it in the mail. If you don't return the proxy, your votes aren't counted.

Usually you'll receive one vote for each share of stock you own. For some big companies the process can be quite complicated. Take AT&T, for instance. With more than 2.4 million stockholders and 1.3 billion shares of stock in circulation, the company's elections involve a lot of vote counting.

HOW CAN YOU RESEARCH A COMPANY WHOSE STOCK YOU MIGHT WANT TO BUY?

You can get a certain amount of information by reading the stock tables in the newspaper. But for real answers, you need to get information from your broker, from other financial media, or from the annual report of the company itself. There are four important questions to be answered.

What's the company's book value? The book value is simply the difference between a company's assets and its liabilities. If a company has a low book value, it can mean that even if it performs well, an inordinate amount of its profits may have to be used to pay off debt. On the other hand, sometimes a low book value is caused by a company's assets being undervalued. In this case, say many experts, its stock is a good buy.

What are the earnings per share? This is easily calculated by dividing a company's profit by the number of shares in the company. A company that's growing will show a steady increase of earnings per share.

What's the return on equity? This figure can be calculated by dividing a company's earnings per share by its book value.

What's the payout ratio? Or, what percentage of its net earnings is the company paying its investors in dividends? Normally, the payout ratio is between 25 and 50 percent. If it's higher, it may mean the company isn't earning enough to meet its obligations and still have a healthy profit left over.

Corporate Reports

Every year publicly held companies issue quarterly and annual reports for their stockholders. Quarterly reports are brief summaries of a company's financial performance for the quarter. They're basically compilations of figures on sales, costs, and earnings.

Annual reports, on the other hand, are quite a bit more elaborate and detailed. They're usually handsomely designed and printed with four-color photography. They include a message from the chairman of the board of directors and maybe one or two other officers. There's also usually a section discussing the company's philosophy, its highlights from the past year, its plans for the future, and specific short- and long-term challenges it may be facing.

A section with financial information will include a profit-and-loss statement and a balance sheet showing assets and liabilities at the end of the year. Finally, there's usually a letter from auditors with an outside accounting firm stating that they have examined the financial statements and find them accurate.

Annual reports are fair and accurate pictures of a company's past performance. But keep in mind that they're prepared by the company itself and therefore will show the company in the best possible light.

The Financial Press

Financial publications will provide you with a more objective look at corporations and investing. Among financial newspapers, the *Wall Street Journal* is the most respected and widely read. It provides exhaustive coverage of the markets and provides up-to-the-minute news on the nation's corporations. It's a must for anyone who follows the markets on a daily basis. *Barron's* is another excellent resource.

Among magazines, *Fortune* and *Forbes* provide the best coverage of corporate America. For investing, particularly for the small investor, magazines like *Money* are the best sources of information.

ARE OVERSEAS COMPANIES WORTHY INVESTMENTS?

By all means. In fact, many investment experts feel that a truly diverse investment portfolio should include a certain number of overseas investments.

One reason is the potential financial reward they offer. Let's say you buy 100 shares of a company in Germany. In a perfect world, the stock price will rise, providing a capital gain, and you also will receive generous dividends. These are the goals of any stock investment, domestic or international.

But there's another factor at play with overseas investments that doesn't exist with domestic stocks—the exchange rate. If, while the price of the stock is rising, the value of the German mark rises against the dollar, you'll receive even more dollars when you sell the stock. On the other hand, if the mark loses value against the dollar, you'll receive fewer dollars, and your profit from the rise in the stock price can be negated. You can even lose money if the mark loses enough value.

So with overseas stocks, there are three main factors that affect profitability—stock price, dividend, and exchange rate. Other factors include differing taxes on capital gains and losses and the expense of converting dividends into dollars. An overseas investment also can be risky because the information available on a company's financial condition may be less complete than that for a domestic company. Also, giving buy and sell orders can be difficult because of language barriers and distance.

FOR MORE INFORMATION

Here are some books for additional research into stocks and investing in stocks.

- *How the Stock Market Works* by John M. Walton, New York Institute of Finance, New York, 1993.
- *A Random Walk Down Wall Street: Including a Life Cycle Guide to Personal Investing* by Burton G. Malkiel, Norton, New York, 1996.
- *Straight Talk About Stock Investing* by John Slatter, McGraw-Hill, New York, 1994.
- *20 Ways You Lose Money On Your Way to the Stock Market* by Scott S. Fraser, Dearborn Trade, 1996.

WHAT'S NEXT

Stocks aren't the only way to invest for your child's college education. Another common investment strategy is to lend your money to a company or institution. In return, the borrower promises to pay you a certain amount in interest while it has your money, issuing you a promissory note that describes the terms of the agreement. These are called bonds. We'll take a look at them in chapter 5.

5

BONDS—THE INVESTOR AS CREDITOR

Bonds are different from stocks. Rather than gaining equity in a company from buying a small chunk of it, as you do when you buy stocks, you become a creditor by lending your money to the company. In return, the issuer agrees to pay you a certain rate of interest at regular intervals during a specified time. At the end of that period, when the bond "matures," you get back the money you paid for the bond to reinvest.

So a bond is essentially an IOU, a promise from the institution to pay back the loan. Bond interest rates are guaranteed and are competitive with the rates of return of other investments.

For years, investors who purchased bonds were issued a certificate with the name of the bond's issuer, its price (also called "par" value), the interest rate, an identifying number, and the date the bond matures. The bond also carried coupons that the investor would tear off and redeem to receive interest payments. For this reason, the interest rate of bonds is often called the "coupon rate."

This changed in the mid-'80s. Although there are still millions of bond certificates in circulation, most new bonds today are registered and stored electronically. These are called "book-entry" bonds.

Bonds are most often sold in multiples of $1,000. Because they pay a guaranteed rate of return over a finite period of time (they're sometimes referred to as "fixed-income" securities), bonds are an enormously popular investment. In fact, Americans have more money invested in bonds than in any other type of security, including stocks and mutual funds.

Bonds are most advantageous as investments for college when interest rates are either relatively stable or in decline and inflation is low. Careful planning is critical when purchasing bonds. It's important to make sure you can keep a bond until maturity and won't need the money for something else. The problem is that bonds may decrease in value when interest rates increase. If you have to sell a bond before it matures and interest rates are high, you may actually lose money.

WHY ARE BONDS ISSUED?

Bonds are commonly issued by corporations, cities, counties, states, and the federal government to raise money for all sorts of things. Corporations use them to acquire capital for expansion and to cover operating costs. Municipal, county, and state governments use them to help pay for roads and bridges, schools, athletic facilities, sewer and water systems, and other capital-intensive projects. The federal government issues bonds to cover the costs of government activities and to help pay off the national debt. It has also issued bonds to finance war efforts. In fact, the first federal bonds were issued in 1790 to pay off Revolutionary War debt. Overseas governments and corporations also offer bonds to American investors.

For a corporation, raising capital by issuing bonds is often preferable to offering additional stock in the company. This is because offering new stock can dilute the value of existing stock and make for some very unhappy stockholders. Governments, on the other hand, have no other option. As non-profit institutions, they are unable to sell stock, so they have to borrow capital. Bonds are a very convenient way to raise money.

HOW LONG IS THE LIFE OF A BOND?

It varies. Some short-term bonds mature in a year or less. The term of intermediate bonds can be from a year to 10 years. Long-term bonds are usually for 30 or more years. In fact one of the most popular bonds is the 30-year treasury bond (often called the "long bond") offered by the U.S. government. But the granddaddy of bonds is probably the 100-year corporate bond first issued by the Disney Corporation in 1993. It will come due in 2093.

ARE BONDS ALWAYS GOOD INVESTMENTS?

Not necessarily. They're certainly safe investments, because the interest rate is guaranteed. But what happens if interest rates start to climb? Let's say you bought a five-year bond that pays 6 percent and two years later interest rates have climbed to 9 percent. You'll lose out because you'll be stuck with your 6 percent interest rate.

On the other hand, if you bought your bond when interest rates were at 9 percent and rates begin to decline, you'll feel like a regular Warren Buffet. While people investing in certificates of deposit and other securities are limping along with their 5 or 6 percent return, you're fat and happy with your 9 percent.

But perhaps the biggest problem with bonds is their vulnerability to inflation. Sure, your interest is guaranteed. But if inflation begins to increase rapidly, it erodes the value of the money the bond is generating. For example, if you buy a bond that returns 9 percent and the rate of inflation stays at 3 percent, you're realizing a real return of 6 percent. But if you have a bond that's returning 6 percent and inflation reaches 6 percent, the value of the return is negated by the inflation. Your investment is flat. If inflation goes higher than 6 percent, you're actually losing money. Keep in mind, too, that college tuitions have been increasing faster than the rate of inflation for some time now. You won't be too happy with an investment that doesn't appreciate at least as quickly.

HOW MUCH CAN YOU EARN?

This also varies. Bond interest rates are comparable to the rates of return from other investments at the time the bonds are issued. They're also tied to length of the life of the bond. Generally, the longer the life of the bond, the higher its rate of return.

Of course, as you'll see in a moment, you also can make money selling bonds before they come due. But this is only possible under certain market conditions.

CAN BONDS BE SOLD BEFORE THEY MATURE?

Sure. In fact, there's a huge bond market on Wall Street that buys and sells millions of bonds every day. Many banks and all the big securities firms have bond trading rooms that operate with all the frenzy of the trading floor on one of the nation's stock exchanges. All this activity is due to the fact that the value of bonds fluctuates as interest rates rise and fall. This fluctuation is inverse in nature—as interest rates decline, the value of existing bonds increases, and vice versa.

When interest rates fall, bonds issued during periods of higher interest rates become very much in demand, and investors will pay a premium to buy them. The purchasers aren't necessarily concerned with the interest that trickles from the bonds over time, even though it's higher than prevailing interest rates. Often they're betting that interest rates will fall further and the value of the bonds they bought last month or last week or just yesterday will increase and they can sell them for a profit.

So, for example, if you've been holding a bond that's been paying a good return for several years and interest rates begin to dip, you can sell the bond for more than its par value. The difference between what you paid for the bond and what you receive for it, combined with the interest you've already earned, can amount to a tidy profit.

But when interest rates start to shoot up (and inflation is usually along for the ride, too), bond prices decrease. If you hold a bond that's earning less than current interest rates, you won't be able to sell it for par value. And the bigger the gap between the two interest rates, the lower the price you'll get for the bond. If its value falls far enough, it can wipe out whatever interest income you might have earned while you owned the bond.

As you can see, interest rates and inflation are important considerations when looking at bonds as long-term investments. If analysts are predicting a rise in inflation and interest rates, you'll be better off putting your money elsewhere.

CAN THE ISSUER OF A BOND PAY BACK INVESTORS EARLY?

Yes, if so stipulated beforehand. This is a process called "redemption" and is a strategy bond issuers use to take advantage of falling interest rates. If rates begin to fall, the issuer can "call" outstanding bonds, pay off the bondholders, and issue new bonds at a lower rate. Almost all corporate bonds and some municipal bonds are callable, but most treasury bonds are not. Nor are treasury bills and agency bonds.

For investors, callable bonds carry an obvious risk. If you have to redeem a bond that's earning 8 percent and then can only earn 5 or 6 percent when you get your original investment back, you're going to be more than just a bit annoyed. For your protection, most callable bonds have provisions stipulating that they can't be called before a certain number of years.

HOW DO YOU CALCULATE A BOND'S VALUE?

The value of a bond is determined by the income it generates. The income, also called "yield," is determined by what you pay for the bond and the bond's interest rate. If you buy a 10-year $1,000 bond with an interest rate of 6.75 percent, you'll earn $67.50 annually. To figure the yield, use this simple equation:

$$\frac{\text{annual interest income}}{\text{price}} = \text{yield}$$

or

$$\frac{\$67.50}{\$1{,}000} = 6.75\% \text{ yield}$$

As you can see, at par value a bond's yield and its interest rate are the same. But if you start buying bonds on the secondary market and paying above or below par value, the yield and the interest rate differ. Let's say you buy the same $1,000 bond two years after issue in a low-interest market and pay $1,150 for it. In this case the math would be as follows:

$$\frac{\$67.50}{\$1{,}150} = 6\% \text{ yield}$$

So in this case, the $150 premium you paid for the bond reduces its yield to 6 percent. Conversely, if you pay below par value (let's say $900) for the bond because interest rates are high, you figure the yield this way:

$\frac{\$67.50}{\$900}$=8% yield

When assessing a bond's value keep in mind that the yield is just part of the picture. The other is the total return on investment, or, assuming you hold the bond until it matures, the "yield-to-maturity." The factors determining yield-to-maturity are the yield, the par value of the bond and the price you actually pay for the bond. Assuming you kept the bonds until maturity, the two scenarios above would provide quite different returns. In the case where you paid the premium price of $1,150 for the bond, you would calculate your return as follows:

$67.50 (interest) ∞ 8 (years until maturity)	$540
Plus par value at maturity	+$1,000
Total return	$1,540
Less cost of bond	-$1,150
Net return on investment	$390

But for the discounted bond, the numbers are quite a bit better:

$67.50 (interest) ∞ 8 (years until maturity)	$540
Plus par value at maturity	+$1,000
Total return	$1,540
Less cost of bond	-$900
Net return on investment	$640

Note, too, that in both cases if you reinvest the interest the bond earns each year, that interest compounded over eight years would make the total return on investment even higher.

ARE SOME BONDS MORE RISKY THAN OTHERS?

Does the name Michael Milken ring a bell? The financial genius who's now Wall Street's most famous ex-con? If it does, you know the answer to this one.

There is indeed a fair amount of risk associated with some

bonds. We've already seen how fluctuating interest rates can hurt the value of a bond. An even bigger risk is not being paid the interest on a bond when it's due or, even worse, not being paid back your investment when the bond matures. If a company goes bankrupt or a municipality or state falls on hard financial times, you may have a hard time getting your money.

To give investors some idea of the risk associated with a particular bond, rating services like Moody's and Standard & Poor's grade bonds according to their risk. They carefully examine the financial health of a bond issuer and then assign its bonds a grade based on the probability of the issuer being able to meet its financial obligations to the bondholders. Corporate and municipal bonds receive most of the attention of rating services. They don't rate U.S. Treasury bonds since they're backed by the federal government and are considered absolutely risk-free.

There are ten grade levels for bonds, ranging from Aaa (Moody's) and AAA (Standard & Poor's) for the highest-quality, lowest-risk bonds to D (Moody's) for the bonds of companies that are in default. Bonds at the upper end of the spectrum are relatively risk-free "investment grade" bonds. Their issuers are considered stable, and your chances of getting stiffed are very slim.

As you move downward through the various grades, however, risk increases. Those at the bottom are the highest risk and include the "junk bonds" made so popular by the infamous Mr. Milken. These are the high-yield bonds that were used to fuel the corporate mergers and takeovers that were so common during the '80s. Unfortunately, billions of dollars were lost by investors who purchased bonds that ended up being worthless.

As you probably have guessed, there is a direct correlation between the risk and yield of a bond. Institutions offering high-grade bonds can offer less interest because their bonds are considered safe and investors will buy them simply to be able to sleep well at night. As you move down in grade, bond issuers need to offer higher interest to attract investors. This is why the yield on junk bonds is so high. But just remember, pigs get slaughtered!

CAN A BOND'S RATING CHANGE?

Yes, and there's really no way you can anticipate it. A company or municipality can suffer a financial downturn. It happens all the time. When it does, the likelihood that an issuer will be unable to pay off its debts increases, so rating services will downgrade its bonds. Existing bonds will decrease in value, and any new bonds the issuer wishes to offer will have to yield higher interest rates.

WHAT ARE THE MOST COMMON TYPES OF BONDS?

As I mentioned earlier, bonds are issued by tens of thousands of corporations, municipalities, and governments. They have varying tax implications and other characteristics that will determine which are most advantageous to your goals.

Municipal Bonds

When a town, city, county, or state needs an infusion of capital to finance a large project like an airport, a stadium, or a school, it will frequently use municipal bonds to generate the money.

Municipal bonds, or "munis," are issued at par values of $5,000 and up. They have one great advantage. To entice investors to buy municipal bonds, which are issued to pay for projects that benefit the public, the federal government exempts the interest they earn from federal taxes. They also are exempt from state taxes, provided the investor is a resident of the same state in which they are issued. Almost all municipal bonds fall within one of two categories:

General obligation bonds (GOs).

These are guaranteed by the issuer and are usually backed by the issuer's full faith and credit. This means when a state or city issues a GO bond, it's guaranteeing the bond with all its resources. It also has the power to impose a tax to cover the cost of repaying bondholders, if necessary. This is why no general obligation bond of a major issuer has defaulted since the depression.

Not all GO bonds have the same risk. When a city or state proposes an issue of GO bonds, analysts evaluate the financial strength of the issuer and then rate the bond. And their ratings can change as the economic fortunes (or misfortunes) of the issuing cities and states change over time. GO bonds also have to be approved by the voters of the state or municipality that intends to issue them.

Revenue bonds.
These bonds pay the money owed bondholders with revenues generated by the project they pay for. Highways, for example, are often paid for with revenue bonds. The tolls paid by motorists are used to pay the interest and the principal on the bonds. Revenue bonds also are used to build airports, stadiums, water and sewer systems, hospitals, public housing, and many other things. They do not require voter approval. Because they carry a slightly higher degree of risk, revenue bonds usually pay slightly higher interest than general obligation bonds.

Some revenue bonds are called moral obligation bonds because there's an implied obligation on the part of the state to guarantee the bonds should the issuing municipality go into default. However, there is no legal obligation on the part of the state to do so.

Are Munis a Good College Investment?

Because of their tax-free aspect, municipal bonds are most popular with investors who are in high-income tax brackets. Although they're not as safe as Treasury securities, they still can be a worthwhile investment for your college fund. Discuss various offerings with your broker. And before you buy, compare prices. You can buy munis through your broker. But you can also buy them through companies who specialize in munis, and their prices are often quite a bit cheaper.

Corporate Bonds

Corporations issue bonds to raise money for all sorts of activities, from expanding their operations or physical plants to bringing new products to market. They generally are divided into four sectors:

- Public utilities, such as telephone companies and power companies
- Transportation companies, including airlines and railroads
- Industrial companies, including both retail and manufacturing companies
- Financial institutions, such as banks and brokerage firms

Corporate bonds can be purchased from brokers, either on an exchange or over-the-counter. They are available in short term (1 to 5 years), intermediate term (5 to 10 years), long term (10 to 20 years) and are sold in $1,000 increments.

Regardless of which sector a corporation is in, its bonds will generally fall into one of two categories: secured (asset-backed) or unsecured (debenture).

Asset-backed bonds.

Companies that issue secured bonds do so by backing them with their assets. They're promising investors that, if they have to, they'll use their equipment, real estate, inventories, and any other assets they have to pay back their bond debt. Essentially, they're putting up their assets as collateral to guarantee loans.

Debenture bonds.

Unsecured bonds are called debenture bonds and are backed solely by the credit of the issuer. Although they sound risky, they're actually quite safe, particularly when issued by a huge company such as General Motors or IBM. A debenture bond from a large, secure corporation is usually less risky than a secured bond from a smaller start-up company. In fact, most corporate bonds are debenture bonds.

Special Types of Corporate Bonds

Within the overall spectrum of corporate bonds, a few have unique qualities.

Zero-coupon bonds.

These are a clever twist on traditional bonds. They're called zero-coupon because they pay the investor no interest (remember, "coupon" means interest in bond lingo) while they're maturing. Instead, the interest accrues and is paid to the investor at maturity.

Because they delay paying interest, zero-coupon bonds are sold at a deep discount to their par value. For example, a $1,000 bond would cost much less than $1,000 but would be worth $1,000 at maturity. At that point, the accumulated interest, combined with the money originally invested in the bond, equals the par value.

Zero-coupon bonds can be excellent investments for your college fund. Careful timing of your bond purchases can result in a series of bonds that mature just as you need the money to pay for tuition each year. There are two serious downsides, however. One, zeros are very volatile in the secondary market, so if you have to sell a bond before maturity, you could be hurt. And two, Uncle Sam doesn't care that you're not receiving your interest every year, so the IRS requires that you pay taxes on the interest you would have received if payments had been made.

Pre-refunded bonds.

These are highly rated bonds whose repayment is guaranteed by the funds from a second bond issue. The whole concept can ring of the "robbing Peter to pay Paul" syndrome, particularly if the company falls on hard times. To eliminate risk, money raised with the second issue is usually invested in risk-free U.S. Treasury securities. Municipal bonds are also sometimes issued as pre-refunded bonds.

Put bonds.

These have a feature that allows the investor to sell them back to the issuer at par value. This protects the investor against a rise in interest rates, which causes bond values to decline. An investor can unload the bond and reinvest the money in a more profitable bond or some other security. The downside to put bonds is that, because they offer the investor an "out," so to speak, they generally provide a lower yield than other bonds.

Floating-rate bonds.

A floating-rate bond is kind of like an adjustable mortgage. The interest rate will fluctuate as market interest rates change. In theory, this prevents a bond from losing value if interest rates rise. In reality, it doesn't always work.

Convertible bonds.

If an investor holds convertible bonds, he can convert them into the issuing corporation's stock at maturity rather than getting a cash repayment. The terms for conversion are set when the bond is issued. It states when the conversion can be made and how many shares of stock each bond will be worth.

High-Risk, High-Yield—the Lure of Junk Bonds

At any given moment, the financial health of individual corporations in the United States is all over the board. Some are riding the crest of record profits. Others are teetering on the brink of extinction and desperately trying to reshape themselves to stay alive.

When companies fall on hard times, rating services downgrade their bonds. If they continue on a downward slide over a period of time, their bond ratings continue to fall with them. During the '70s, the term "junk bonds" was coined to refer to the bonds of companies who had reached the brink of default.

But then in the '80s high-yield junk bonds began to be issued to finance the activities of emerging companies. They were basically a form of the old carrot-and-the-stick approach to motivating people, and they took advantage of that easily manipulated human trait known as greed. Investors knew they were risky, but the promise of such high yields made them ignore the risk. Corporate raiders began to use junk bonds to finance the hostile takeovers of companies that would then be dismantled and sold off piece by piece. A lot of people made unbelievable amounts of money.

Until 1990, junk bonds remained good investments because their default rate was quite low. But then, like the proverbial house of cards, the junk bond market finally began to collapse. Over the next two years, there were more than $50 billion worth of defaults, representing nearly 20 percent of the junk bond market. By the time the dust settled, Drexel Burnham Lambert, Inc., the primary market maker in junk bonds, was bankrupt; Michael Milken, the Drexel executive who was the brain behind junk bonds, was doing soft time in one of the government's "Club Fed" minimum security institutions for white-collar bad boys; and the federal government was bailing out the nation's savings and loan industry from billions of dollars' worth of junk bond losses.

Since then, junk bonds have rebounded and are still being bought and sold. Their high yields will always make them attractive to certain investors (sometimes known as "bottom feeders"), and some people make a lot of money with them. But unless you're willing to become a very serious student of investing and spend a great deal of time following bankruptcy proceedings and the other activities that drive the junk bond market, they're good things to stay away from.

Are Corporate Bonds Good Investments for a College Fund?

Generally, no. They're usually the domain of large institutional traders, not small investors. And even if you do get involved, they have many disadvantages. For one thing, corporate bonds are taxed at every level—federal, state, and local—so they need to produce an enormous yield to compete with bonds that are tax-exempt. They can be called, so you might suddenly find yourself looking for a new and less profitable investment. They also carry more risk than a federally backed bond. If the company issuing the bond has problems, it can affect the value of the bond. If things get bad enough, the bond can end up worthless.

And it's not just the issuing company you have to worry about. Bad news for one company tends to affect all the other companies in the same sector. For example, if a class action suit is brought against a tobacco company, or an airline loses a big liability suit, it can cause a downturn for all tobacco and airline companies.

What to Ask and What to Look For

If you do decide to invest in corporate bonds, there are a number of questions to ask and things to look for. Ask your broker to get you the information you need, and discuss each investment very carefully. Here are some questions to ask:

What's the history of the company? Approach the purchase of a bond just as you would the purchase of a company's stock.

How does the yield on the corporate bond compare with the yield on U.S. Treasury bonds that mature around the same time? If it's not any higher, buy the Treasury bonds. In fact, because of the risk inherent in corporate bonds, it should yield at least a point more than the Treasury bonds for you to consider buying it.

Are these new issue bonds? If they are, the price you pay for them will be close to what institutions are paying.

What's the bond's rating? It should be an A (by both Moody's and Standard & Poor's) or better. Lower-rated bonds carry higher yields but also have a higher chance of default (remember what happens to pigs).

How many other bond issues are senior to the one you're thinking of investing in? In other words, how many other investors have to get their money from the issuer before you get yours?

U.S. TREASURY BONDS

U.S. Treasury securities are sold in three forms—bills, notes, and bonds. They are backed by the federal government and are therefore, virtually risk-free. There is risk involved, however, if the securities are part of a fund and the fund falls victim to mismanagement. (We'll look at bond funds later when we look at mutual funds.)

Treasury securities can be purchased from a bank, a brokerage house, or in the open market. You also can buy them at a Treasury auction by establishing a "Treasury Direct" account with the Federal Reserve Bank. When you make your first purchase, an account is set up for you, and all your subsequent purchases are kept in that account. You can keep up to $100,000 worth of securities in your account without charge. If you have more than that amount, there is a nominal charge of $25 a year.

Using a Treasury Direct account to purchase and store Treasury securities has several advantages. The biggest is the fact that the federal government, not a brokerage firm, is the custodian of your securities, so they're safe. There are no fees imposed on the purchase or sale of securities. When a security matures, you can either have the money wired at no charge directly to a personal account of your choosing or you can have it reinvested in new issues.

There are also a few disadvantages to using Treasury Direct. One is that you can only purchase Treasury securities at auction. If you want to sell them before maturity, you have to first have them transferred to a brokerage firm or a bank, and this causes delays in getting your money. You also can't borrow against securities held in a Treasury Direct account. Again, they first have to be transferred to a brokerage firm or bank.

Treasury securities are liable for federal taxes but are exempt from state and local taxes.

Treasury Bills

These securities, also known as T-bills, are the shortest-term of all Treasury securities. They can have maturity dates of 13 weeks, 26 weeks, or 52 weeks. So investors can buy new issues at any time, 13- and 26-week T-bills are issued at auction every week, on Monday. Fifty-two week T-bills are usually offered quarterly. As with zero-coupon bonds, you pay a discounted rate and then receive the face value of T-bills at maturity. Federal taxes are due in the year they mature.

T-bills are a fairly exotic animal for the small investor. This is because they require a minimum investment of $10,000 with additional purchase increments of $1,000. Generally, they're purchased by the managers of big pension funds, money market funds, corporations, and governments as a safe short-term investment while they consider more long-term plans for their money.

Treasury Notes and Treasury Bonds

These differ from T-bills in two ways. First, they have longer terms to maturity. Treasury notes have maturities of from 1 to 10 years. Treasury bonds mature in 10 to 30 years. The rock-solid 30-year Treasury bond is usually considered the benchmark against which all other bonds are measured.

Second, rather than being offered at a discount, Treasury notes and Treasury bonds are sold at par value, and interest is distributed periodically until maturity. They are usually offered at the Treasury auction quarterly. They can also be purchased in the over-the-counter market. The minimum purchase price of 5-, 10-, and 30-year Treasury notes and Treasury bonds is only $1,000, so they are viable options for a college fund.

Zero-coupon Treasury securities.

When you buy a Treasury bond, you can turn it into a zero-coupon bond by immediately stripping off the interest coupons and selling them to other investors. For example, if you purchase a 10-year $10,000 bond paying 6 percent, and the interest is to be distributed every six months, you will have 20 coupons to sell. At 6 percent, the bond will pay $600 a year, so each coupon will be worth $300 when it's redeemed.

The price you receive from investors for each coupon will vary depending on when the coupon's interest payment is to be made. The sooner a coupon can be redeemed, the more it's worth. The cheapest of the 20 coupons will be the last one cashed in at the same time the bond reaches maturity. For investors who purchase the coupons, each one is like a mini zero-coupon bond. They pay a discount rate for the coupon and then collect its full value at maturity.

Once you've sold the coupons, you're left with a $10,000 zero-coupon bond that will come due in 10 years. You've already received income for the coupons, and that can be reinvested. As with other types of zero-coupon bonds, you'll be liable for the annual federal tax on the income you would have received. You'll be exempt from state and local taxes.

U.S. SAVINGS BONDS

The federal government has issued savings bonds for years. They're different from corporate and municipal bonds because they can't be traded on the secondary market. They're popular as gifts (hint, hint, if any grandparents are reading this), and, because you can buy a savings bond for as little as $25, they're a good place to invest any extra cash you might find from time to time. They can be purchased from banks or directly from the Federal Reserve.

In one way, savings bonds are like zero-coupon bonds. You buy them at a discount to the par value and receive the full amount when the bond matures. Unlike zeros, however, you don't have to pay tax each year on the interest that accrues. Another plus is that when you cash in the bond, you only pay federal taxes on the interest. They're exempt from state and local taxes. Here are some other advantages:

- They are completely risk free. The issuer is the federal government, so the only way you're not going to get paid is if the government falls. And if that happens, you're going to have bigger things on your mind than your savings bonds.
- You can cash them in as soon as six months after purchase and receive some interest.
- You're not stuck with your interest rate. If you can earn a higher return elsewhere, you can cash them in and reinvest your money.
- They're not callable, so you won't have to worry about suddenly having to invest your money at a lower rate.
- You can purchase them monthly through a payroll deduction plan.

Series EE bonds.

The government issues savings bonds in series. Since 1980, it has been issuing Series EE Savings Bonds, and they have proven to be one of the most popular with investors. They can be purchased in denominations of $50, $75, $200, $500, $1,000, $5,000, and $10,000, and you can invest up to $15,000 annually. The bonds' redemption values increase every six months, so to maximize profits it's important to cash them in just after they've passed a six-month point.

For 15 years, EE bonds carried a guaranteed minimum rate of interest. Since May 1995, however, their interest rates have been tied to the performance of Treasury securities. If a bond is held for more than five years before it's cashed in, it will receive interest at 85 percent of the average return on five-year marketable Treasury bonds. If it's held for less than five years, it will only earn the market rates of the six-month Treasury bill. There's a significant difference between the two, so if you can't afford to hold on to a savings bond for at least five years, there are better places to put your money.

What are the advantages of investing in Series EE bonds for college? If you have a child in college and cash in EE bonds to pay tuition, you may not have to pay federal taxes (this also applies to tuition for you and your spouse). This makes EEs a great investment to put in your college portfolio. To take advantage of the tax break, the following conditions must apply:

- The bonds must have been purchased after 1990.
- The bonds must be purchased in the parents' name, not in the child's name.
- Parents must be at least 24 years of age.
- The money from the bonds must be used the same year the bonds are redeemed, and all the money must be used for tuition. It cannot be used for room and board.
- Parents must meet income requirements. In 1996, the adjusted gross income for a married couple had to be $61,850 or less ($41,200 or less for a single parent) to take advantage of the tax break.

Series HH bonds.

When Series EE bonds mature, investors can either cash them in or convert them into another type of savings bond—the Series HH bond. These bonds are issued at face value rather than at a discount, and interest is paid twice a year. The Federal Reserve will either send you a check or deposit the money directly into a bank account. Because interest is paid during the life of the bond, you are responsible for federal taxes on the interest every year.

There is a distinct tax advantage to the conversion strategy. When you convert an EE bond into an HH bond, you don't have to pay taxes on the interest that the bond accrued as an EE. For example, if you cash in an EE bond that you bought for $500 and is now worth $1,000, you will owe taxes on the $500 in interest it's earned. But if you convert the EE bond into an HH bond, you can put off reporting that $500 until you eventually cash in the HH bond. You do, however, begin to pay annual income tax on the interest the HH bond earns.

AGENCY BONDS

Government agencies like the Federal Housing Administration (FHA) and the Federal Farm Credit Bank issue bonds to pay for things like mortgage loans and economic development projects. They generally have higher yields than Treasury bonds and are almost as safe, since they're backed by federal agencies.

Agencies that were formerly administered by the government but are now public corporations also issue bonds. The best known are the Federal National Mortgage Association (Fannie Mae), the Government National Mortgage Association (Ginnie Mae), and the Federal Home Loan Mortgage Corporation (Freddie Mac). Their bonds are backed by the pools of mortgages they issue.

FOR MORE INFORMATION

Here are some books that can help you learn more about bonds.

- *Straight Talk About Bonds and Bond Funds* by Hildy Richelson and Stan Richelson, McGraw Hill, New York, 1996.
- *Bond Markets, Analysis and Strategies* by Frank J. Fabozzi, Prentice-Hall, New York, 1996.

WHAT'S NEXT?

Stocks and bonds will always be enormously popular investments with investors of all kinds, including parents who are building equity to pay for college. Still, as we've learned so many times in the last few chapters, stocks and bonds have varying degrees of risk and can sometimes result in financial disaster.

Wall Street has recognized this fact for years. As a solution, it offers another very popular financial product, the mutual fund.

These are collections of stocks and bonds that are bundled together to help reduce risk and increase the odds of profitability. Like other investments, they must be selected carefully. But the right funds can be great places in which to invest for parents who are saving for college. We'll look at mutual funds in chapter 6.

6

MUTUAL FUNDS—THERE'S STRENGTH IN NUMBERS

One of the keys to successful investing is reducing risk. This is why mutual funds are so popular.

A mutual fund is a group of securities purchased with the pooled resources of many, many investors and overseen by a professional fund manager. In fact, in some ways, a mutual fund is kind of like a big investing club. The investors pool their money and then share in the fund's earnings proportional to their holdings in the fund.

It's basically the "strength in numbers" approach to investing. The theory is that while some of the fund's holdings may not perform well, the majority will do well and the overall value of the fund will increase and generate a good return on investment.

Mutual funds have been part of American investing since 1924, when Massachusetts Investors Trust, the first open-ended mutual fund, was organized. The concept grew slowly, and as recently as 1975 there were fewer than 500 mutual funds available. The last decade, however, has seen the market explode, and more than 25 percent of American households have investments in at least one of the more than 6,000 mutual funds that are now available. All told, more than $1.5 trillion dollars are invested in mutual funds.

WHAT ARE THE BENEFITS OF MUTUAL FUNDS?

There are several. One of the biggest is the fact that decisions affecting mutual funds are made by professional fund managers and not by you. These are people with impeccable financial educations and training whose sole purpose in life is to make the funds they manage earn as much as possible. While you're spending eight or more hours a day at your job, dealing with the kids, running to the store, and trying to find a few moments to keep up with the financial news, they're visiting companies, analyzing financial reports, and tirelessly scouring the horizon for promising places to invest your money.

Fund managers also have a very personal reason to keep their profits high. They're not just working on behalf of you and other investors. Almost all of them receive compensation based on how well their funds perform. The better the funds do, the more money the fund managers make. The best fund managers can earn millions of dollars a year.

Another advantage of mutual funds is their low cost. Because they buy and sell huge volumes of stocks and bonds at a time, their transaction fees are much less than you would pay your broker in commission when buying and selling your own securities. A good stock mutual fund should cost you no more than 1 percent of your investment every year in service fees. Mutual funds also provide a level of diversification that's almost impossible for the small investor to achieve. To minimize risk, a good mutual fund will have investments in a dozen or more securities. This allows the fund to withstand downturns in individual industries. Unless you have many thousands of dollars to invest, it's very difficult to create a personal portfolio with that sort of built-in protection.

But for parents investing for college, perhaps the best thing about mutual funds is the ability to pick and choose from an enormous selection of funds that meet their investment goals. For example, those parents with a lot of time until their child enters college might invest in aggressive growth funds. They have time on their side and can weather the risk associated with such funds.

Parents with less time to save, however, might want to pursue a more conservative investment path. They need a more reliable return and can invest in funds that are designed to provide exactly that.

DO YOU NEED A LOT OF MONEY TO INVEST IN MUTUAL FUNDS?

No. Most of them have low minimum investment requirements. And the nice thing is that once your money is included in the fund, it's receiving the same careful attention that's being given to the money of the fund's biggest investors. Remember, in a mutual fund, all the investors are in it together, and what's good for one is good for all.

HOW DO YOU EARN MONEY WITH MUTUAL FUNDS?

Mutual funds earn income for their investors in three ways—payment of dividends received from the securities held by the fund, payment of capital gains realized from trading securities in the fund, and increases in the price of their shares. The sum of these three is the total return on a fund.

Dividends are paid either as cash or as additional shares in the fund. But when dividends are paid, the price of the shares in the fund drops by the amount needed to offset the amount of the dividends paid out. Dividend income, whether received in cash or reinvested in additional shares, is considered taxable income.

Capital gains are the net profits realized during the year by fund managers buying and selling securities in a mutual fund. They are usually paid out to investors at the end of each calendar year. As with dividends, capital gains can be received either as cash or as additional shares in the fund; the price of the shares in the fund will decrease to offset the capital gains distribution; and they are taxable whether received as cash or as additional shares.

Fund share prices fluctuate with dividend and capital gains payouts and with the infusion of capital from new investors into the fund. At some point, the share price may be less than you paid (although this will be offset by profit in the form of dividend and capital gains payouts), and at other times it may be more than you paid.

WHAT DO MUTUAL FUNDS INVEST IN?

Most novice investors assume that all mutual funds invest only in stocks. In fact, mutual funds invest in three types of securities—stocks, bonds, and money markets. Some invest in a combination of stocks and bonds. A little less than half of all mutual funds are stock funds. The rest are divided equally between bond funds and money market funds.

Stock funds, also called equity funds, invest in stocks and are usually categorized by the type of stocks they invest in. They may invest in small, medium, or large companies. They may also invest in either growth stocks, whose companies are enjoying high revenues and profits, or value stocks, whose prices are bargains compared to the assets and profits of the company.

Because stock prices are inherently volatile, stock funds are generally considered to be the riskiest of the three types of mutual funds. Still, in a boom market like the one that's existed in the '90s, a well-managed fund will make a lot of investors very happy people.

Bond funds invest in a variety of bonds that have similar maturities. They can be short term (2 to 3 years), intermediate term (5 to 10 years), or long term (20 years or more). Bond fund managers constantly shift the bonds they manage to maintain the fund's desired average maturity. Because bond interest rates are usually guaranteed, bond mutual funds carry less risk than stock funds.

Money market funds are the safest of all mutual funds. In fact, they're virtually risk-free. The fund assets are put in short-term money market investments. Like a savings account, you get back your investment plus whatever interest it earns.

During the '90s, as the stock market has soared to one record high after another and interest rates have remained fairly stable, money market funds have not been very profitable. However, if you're a novice investor with little money, they're a good place to get started. As you build equity, you can begin to direct some of your money to more aggressive stock and bond funds.

Hybrid funds invest in both stocks and bonds. A stock fund, for example, might actually have 10 or 20 percent of its holdings in bonds. This is done to further minimize risk in times of economic downturn. Because bond interest rates are guaranteed, the bonds in the fund will help the fund maintain its value if the stock market goes into decline. Of course, the other side of the coin is that the bonds can hold the fund back somewhat when the stock market is booming.

Index funds are a safe, if not very creative, strategy for investing in mutual funds. They're safe because they're managed to mimic an existing market index, so they're guaranteed to never perform worse than that market. For example, one of the most popular index funds is based on the Standard and Poor's 500, an index of 500 large U.S. companies.

What's so great about matching the market? Well, if you're one of the many, many fund managers whose funds don't perform up to the market every year, it seems like a wonderful accomplishment. Keep in mind that for every mutual fund that enjoys a 20 or 25 percent rate of return, there are a bunch earning only 4 or 5 or 6 percent. There are also some that are actually losing money. So matching the market is not that bad a deal in the overall scheme of things. In fact, over periods of 10 years or more, index funds outperform 75 percent of all other mutual funds.

One reason index funds perform well is the low cost of operating them. Most use computers to make their investment decisions and aren't burdened with analysts and managers and their expensive salaries and offices and other expenses. This allows the funds to charge a fraction of what other mutual funds charge in annual fees. The difference is passed on to investors.

Of course, since index funds are geared to match the market, they're only good investments when the market is performing well. When the market is in a downturn, investors look for other places to put their money.

Tax-free funds are funds that pay tax-free distributions. They accomplish this by investing in things like tax-free municipal bonds and selling the mutual funds created with those bonds to residents of the states in which the bonds are issued.

Security funds, also known as sector funds, invest in securities in specific industries, such as communications or manufacturing. They're odd creatures because they really fly in the face of the whole rationale behind mutual funds. Rather than pursue diversification to reduce risk, they put all their eggs into one basket in the hope that the industry they've chosen will enjoy a boom period.

It's a gamble. If they're right, they make a lot of money. If they're wrong, they lose big time. For this reason, security funds are not for the average investor. And they're certainly not for parents who are saving for college.

DO MUTUAL FUNDS INVEST SOLELY IN U.S. SECURITIES?

No. In fact, many aggressive, high-growth mutual funds are now looking overseas for new opportunities. These funds usually have names like the Acme Global Equity Fund or the ABC International Growth Fund. Those funds with the word "international" in their name generally focus solely on non-U.S. investments. Those with "worldwide" or "global" in their name may invest in both U.S. and overseas investments. However, the only real way to determine where a fund is investing is to contact the fund managers themselves.

These kinds of funds are generally not for people who are investing for their children's college educations. For one thing, following markets in different parts of the world is very difficult for a fund manager, so the risk is higher. The instability of individual governments may negatively impact some of the companies these funds invest in. Overseas funds also charge more in service fees than domestic mutual funds do.

HOW RISKY ARE MUTUAL FUNDS?

Like other investments, mutual funds have varying degrees of risk. It depends on the types of securities they invest in. They also have a level of return commensurate with the amount of risk they carry. The most common types of mutual funds are listed below, from highest risk to lowest.

Small capitalization funds are the most aggressive of all mutual funds. They invest in the stocks of young companies that have the potential for rapid growth. Because they have a high potential return, they also carry the most risk. If you like a wild ride and the excitement of watching an investment rise and fall like a kite on a windy day, this type of fund will provide it. Because of their potential volatility, small capitalization funds are good investments for people whose children are quite young and who can hold on to an investment for a number of years.

Growth funds are also designed to pursue a high rate of return and carry a similar level of risk. But rather than invest in small start-up companies, they buy the stock of larger, more established companies.

Growth and income funds are more conservative than small capitalization funds and growth funds. They are designed to provide a good return, but to reduce risk they invest in both stocks and bonds. Their share values tend to be more stable than those of growth funds. Because they're designed to provide income as well as growth, they usually pay a lower return.

Income funds are even less risky. They're designed to guarantee an income and generally invest in bonds.

Tax-exempt funds are also designed to guarantee an income. They invest in securities that are exempt from federal income taxes, such as municipal bonds. The level of risk is quite low.

Money market funds are the most risk-free of mutual funds. They also generally provide the lowest return.

As an individual investor, you'll need to decide what your financial goals are and what levels of risk you're most comfortable with. If you have a long period of time until your child enters college, you might decide that you're comfortable with aggressive growth funds. You'll certainly have the time to weather the ups and downs of the market. On the other hand, if you've already managed to put together a considerable nest egg and are looking for minimal risk and are content to live with a lower return, bond funds, tax-exempt funds, and money market funds may be your best strategy.

If you have less time to invest until college arrives, it's more of a crap shoot. You can shoot for the moon by selecting aggressive growth funds and hope they perform well and that you can maximize your return. Or you may decide to play it safe and go for the guaranteed income offered by less risky funds.

HOW DO YOU INVESTIGATE MUTUAL FUNDS?

As I mentioned earlier in the chapter, there are more than 6,000 mutual funds available to today's investor. They range from high-risk, small capitalization funds to safe-as-milk money market funds. Some perform admirably and make their investors a lot of money. Others are the butt of jokes up and down Wall Street.

When you begin to investigate different mutual funds, you'll come across all sorts of confusing information. If you're dealing with a broker who's more interested in making a sale than in helping you choose the most appropriate fund for your goals, you may be told all sorts of stories. Even no-load funds purchased directly from a mutual fund company can be confusing.

How can you be sure the fund or funds you select are safe investments and meet your investment goals? Unfortunately, there are no guarantees. But by following a few simple guidelines and asking the right questions you can minimize your risk and maximize your chances for investment success.

The best way to get a clear picture of a mutual fund is the prospectus. This is a legally mandated document that describes in detail everything about the fund. It's reviewed by the Securities and Exchange Commission before it's allowed to be distributed to investors, and it contains answers to the following questions.

What Does the Fund Invest In?

The prospectus will state what sort of securities the fund invests in and what the fund's goals are. For example, one fund might invest in U.S. treasury bonds and blue-chip corporate bonds with the goal of providing a steady, risk-free income. Another might invest in a combination of stocks and bonds to provide both income and growth. Still another might invest in high-risk junk bonds in an attempt to provide the highest possible income.

How Is the Fund Operated?

The prospectus also describes the policies and procedures the fund uses in pursuing its investment goals. Investors have a stake in these issues and are allowed to vote on proposed major changes in fund policy. For example, mutual funds will sometimes borrow money to augment the amount contributed by investors. If the fund managers intend to change the amount they're allowed to borrow, they must receive the approval of the fund's investors. This is accomplished with a vote much like that carried out by the shareholders in a corporation. You can cast your vote either in person or by proxy.

What's the Minimum Investment Required by the Fund?

Mutual funds have minimum investment requirements. Most are quite low, sometimes as little as $500. The minimum required for opening an account is always higher than the minimum required to add to an account.

What Are the Costs Associated with the Fund?

Mutual funds assess their investors a variety of charges for buying and selling the fund. There are also operating expenses that are passed on to the investors. These charges can put a big dent in the income you receive, so it's critical that you find out up front what these costs are before you invest.

Loads are commissions paid to brokers who sell mutual funds. They can be anywhere from 4 to 8.5 percent (the maximum allowed by law). If we translate that into the commission on a $5,000 investment, we're talking about anywhere from $200 to $425 that's essentially deducted from the value of your investment right off the bat. It's a big chunk of money that will take some time to make up.

No-load funds, on the other hand, don't charge a commission. There are plenty of good ones out there, and there's really no reason to invest in a fund that does charge a commission. The problem is you can't necessarily trust a broker if he or she tells you there are no load charges associated with a fund. Often, the charge is buried within the operating expenses, which will be inflated to make sure the broker gets the commission.

Operating expenses are the annual charges a fund assesses its investors to cover its own costs. Mutual funds are fairly expensive to maintain. They require office space, computers and telecommunications equipment, office staff, portfolio managers and analysts, advertising, accountants, and the preparation of countless documents.

Over the last decade, as more and more funds have been created, operating expenses have increased. Twenty years ago, most funds charged around 0.5 percent of their average annual assets. Today, operational fees for new funds are usually set at from 0.75 to 1 percent of average assets. That figure can change, however, as the fund grows. Overall, operational expenses range from 0.2 percent to 1.3 percent, depending on the type of fund.

Distribution fees are assessed to cover the costs of marketing and advertising a fund. About half of all funds charge them.

Redemption fees are charged investors when they sell their shares in a fund. Some redemption fees, known as deferred sales loads, are charged only during a specified time, such as the first three years an investor is in a fund. After that, no redemption fee will be assessed when shares are sold.

Reinvestment fees are assessed when investors choose to have their dividends and capital gains payments reinvested in the fund in the form of additional shares.

Exchange fees are assessed when investors transfer money from one mutual fund to another.

How Has the Fund Performed over Time?

The performances of mutual funds are all over the board. Some do unbelievably well for short periods of time and then flame out quickly. Others are slow and steady winners that chug along reliably like the Energizer Bunny. Still others fluctuate, performing admirably for a few years and then slumping for a period of time before bouncing back.

Even though past performance is no guarantee of future profitability, the history of a mutual fund can give you some idea of what to expect. When you're evaluating various funds, look at their performance over a 5-to-10 year period. This will give you some idea of how they match up to your investment goals. Another good way to measure their performance is to compare them to various market indexes. Compare stock funds to the Standard & Poor's 500, bond funds to one of the many bond indexes that exist, and so on. If a fund has consistently outperformed the market, it's definitely worth serious consideration.

Is It an Open-end or Close-end Fund?

Some mutual funds are allowed to grow by selling as many shares as the market will bear. As more shares are added to a fund, the fund manager has more capital to work with. These are called open-end funds. Although in theory they are limitless in size, they will in fact grow to a point where they become too unwieldy to manage, and no additional investors are allowed on board. Existing investors, however, can continue to put money into the fund.

Other funds, however, are created with a predetermined number of shares and, like stocks, are traded on an exchange. These are called close-end funds, and their prices fluctuate with investor demand.

What's the Fund's Turnover Rate?

The shares of open-end mutual funds are bought and sold just like stocks. The turnover rate tells investors how much actual trading is going on each year. Some funds experience very little turnover. Others can experience a whopping 100 percent ratio. High turnovers generally mean higher costs.

How Can Shares Be Bought and Sold?

The prospectus describes the procedures for buying and selling shares. You can buy mutual funds from brokers (to be avoided if at all possible because of the commission) or directly through companies that offer mutual funds (some of these have front end charges, too).

Once you've decided on the fund or funds you want to invest in, you complete a purchase application similar to the form you'd fill out to open a checking account. If you're buying directly from a fund company, you send them the application, along with a check for the amount you're investing. If you're buying from a broker, you'll also need to include the commission.

Once you've opened your account, most funds allow you to simply make a phone call to make subsequent investments. You can even arrange for periodic direct deposits from a designated account if you want to make continuous investments in the fund over time.

What Services Does the Fund Offer?

Most mutual funds offer features such as wire transfer privileges, check-writing privileges, and a cash withdrawal option.

WHAT OTHER INFORMATION SHOULD YOU LOOK FOR?

The prospectus offers a pretty comprehensive look at a mutual fund, but there are a couple of questions it won't answer. To get the answers, you'll need to do some research in the financial media and ask the appropriate people, including your accountant.

What's the Reputation of the Fund Manager and the Fund Family?

Over the years, the astonishing success of some mutual funds has given their managers the kind of celebrity usually reserved for athletes and rock stars. The financial press covers their every move, and the mere mention of their names can cause serious mutual fund devotees to swoon. Perhaps the most famous fund manager was Peter Lynch, who managed Fidelity's Magellan Fund for 15 years. During that time, the fund averaged an amazing 30.5 percent annual return.

There's no question that the reputation of a fund manager is important. But equally important are the resources behind the manager. Different companies have strengths in different types of mutual funds. Some are known for their stock funds. Others are specialists in bond and money market funds. A little research into the resources and strengths of various companies and their fund managers will help you make informed investment decisions.

What Are the Tax Implications of the Fund?

Many mutual fund investors fail to consider the tax implications of the funds they invest in. This is a big mistake, because taxes can cut heavily into your net earnings from a fund. After-tax earnings are your real bottom line, not pre-tax earnings.

The problem is that some mutual funds produce more taxable gains than others, and the taxes on those gains diminish the actual return. Your goal as an investor should be to look for funds that minimize capital gains distributions. This allows your money to compound as it would in an IRA or other retirement account, in addition to letting you defer taxes.

Some fund representatives will be able to discuss this issue with you. You also might want to consult with an accountant familiar with mutual funds.

SHOULD YOU INVEST IN MORE THAN ONE MUTUAL FUND?

Yes, if you have the resources. Just as investing in one mutual fund helps reduce risk, investing in several reduces risk even further. You might want to put some money in a stock fund, some in a bond fund, and some in a hybrid fund that contains both stock and bonds. You might even want to invest in an index fund. It depends on your goals, your affinity for risk, and how long you have to save for college.

Many mutual fund companies offer a wide choice of funds that reflect various levels of risk and offer investments in a variety of stocks, bonds, and money markets. These have come to be known as mutual fund "families" and provide investors with a wide range of services. Investing with one of these families provides simplified statements that show the status of all your accounts.

If you have money in several mutual funds managed by one company, it's easy to move your money around from one fund to another. In most cases, a phone call to an 800 number is all it takes. This allows you to make changes in your mutual fund holdings in response to changing market conditions.

Following is a list of 26 major mutual fund families and their addresses and phone numbers.

Alliance Capital Management
500 Plaza Dr.
Secaucus, NJ 07094
800-221-5672
• Offers mostly load funds with a variety of payment options.

American Capital
P.O. Box 3528
Houston, TX 77253
800-421-5666
• Old, established firm with high loads but also some of the best-performing funds in the country.

Babson
2440 Pershing Rd.
3 Crown Center
Kansas City, MO 64108
800-422-2766
• Offers no-load funds and specializes in managing equity portfolios.

Benham Group
1665 Charleston Rd.
Mountain View, CA 94043
800-472-3389
• Offers no-load funds and is known for its selection of fixed-income funds.

Capital Research and Management
333 S. Hope St., 52nd Floor
Los Angeles, CA 90071
800-421-9900

- Established, solid, and conservative. Known for its large research department and multi-manager approach to fund management.

Columbia
1301 S.W. 5th Ave.
P.O. Box 1350
Portland, OR 97207
800-547-1707

- No-load, employee-owned company known for its equity funds and team approach to fund management.

Dodge & Cox
1 Sansome
San Francisco, CA 94104
415-434-0311

- Offers only three funds but has a long history of success with its value-oriented, diversified approach.

Evergreen Funds
2500 Westchester Ave.
Purchase, NY 10577
800-235-0064

- No-loads offered by experts in small capitalization funds.

Fidelity Investments
82 Devonshire St.
Boston, MA 02109
800-544-8888

- The nation's largest mutual fund company is known for its innovative management and offers investors more than 100 different funds.

Founders
2930 E. 3rd Ave.
Denver, CO 80206
800-342-5236

- Small, well-run company offers nine funds and a progressive management style.

Franklin/Templeton Funds
777 Mariners Island Blvd.
San Mateo, CA 94403
800-342-5236
• Specializes in fixed-income funds and usually charges loads.

IAI Group
3700 First Bank Place
P.O. Box 357
Minneapolis, MN 55440
800-945-3863
• Conservative company specializing in domestic and international equity funds.

INVESCO Funds Group
P.O. Box 2040
Denver, CO 80217
800-525-8085
• Established company best known for its conservative equity funds.

Janus Group
100 Fillmore St.
Suite 300
Denver, CO 80206
800-525-3713
• Very successful company with a real talent for managing domestic equity funds.

Mutual Series Funds
51 JFK Parkway
Short Hills, NJ 07078
800-448-3863
• Offers four funds and has a knack for investing in troubled companies with undervalued stock.

Neuberger & Berman
605 3rd Ave., 2nd Floor
New York, NY 10158
800-877-9700
• Conservative, value-oriented firm with an impeccable track record, no-loads, and low expenses.

Nicholas Funds
700 N. Water St.
Suite 1010
Milwaukee, WI 53202
414-272-6133

• Offers no-load funds, low maintenance fees, and invests for the long haul.

Nuveen
333 W. Wacker Dr.
Chicago, IL 60606
800-351-4100

• Specializes solely in tax-free funds and unit investments trusts, which are marketed by brokerage firms and other financial institutions.

SAFECO
P.O. Box 34890
Seattle, WA 98124
800-624-5711

• No-loads with a conservative, value-oriented philosophy.

Scudder
160 Federal St., 12th Floor
Boston, MA 02100
800-225-2470

• This large company created the first no-load fund in 1928 and is still solely no-load.

SteinRoe
P.O. Box 1162
Chicago, IL 60690
800-338-2550

• Low-profile company offers well-managed, no-load funds.

Strong Funds
100 Heritage Reserve
Menomonee Falls, WI 53201
800-368-3863

• Actively managed funds known for seeking a combination of income and capital appreciation.

T. Rowe Price
100 E. Pratt St.
Baltimore, MD 21202
800-638-5660
- No-load funds offered by a company famed for its customer service.

Twentieth Century
4500 Main St.
P.O. Box 418210
Kansas City, MO 64111
800-345-2021
- Offers risky but profitable equity funds.

United Funds
6300 Lamar Ave.
P.O. Box 29217
Shawnee Mission, KS 66201
913-236-2000
- Conservatively managed funds with fairly high front-end loads.

Vanguard Group
Vanguard Financial Center
Valley Forge, PA 19482
800-635-1511
- Huge firm, completely no-load with low maintenance charges and a taste for index funds.

FOR MORE INFORMATION

The following books can help you learn more about mutual funds.

- *A Commonsense Guide to Mutual Funds* by Mary Rowland, Bloomberg Press, Princeton, New Jersey, 1996.
- *Mutual Funds Made Easy* by Gerald W. Perritt, Dearborn Financial Publishing, Inc., Chicago, 1995.
- *How Mutual Funds Work* by Albert J. Fredman and Russ Wiles, New York Institute of Finance, New York, 1993.

WHAT'S NEXT?

Stocks, bonds, and mutual funds are the three most common investment strategies for people who are saving for all sorts of things, including college. But they're not the only choices out there.

For those people who are somewhat investment-savvy going into the process, or have become more savvy through their own self-education, investments like futures and options can offer additional ways to make money. They're not for the novice, but if you know what you're doing they're worth checking out. We'll take a look at them in chapter 7.

7

FUTURES AND OPTIONS—HIGH RISK, HIGH REWARD

The fertile imagination of the investment world has created many investment vehicles other than stocks, bonds, and mutual funds. Many are too esoteric and confusing for the average investor and are particularly inappropriate for someone who's attempting to put money aside for college. But two—futures and options—are worth examining.

Be forewarned, however. Futures and options are high-risk investment strategies that can make you a bundle but could also cause you to lose your shirt. The mechanisms affecting them must be well understood before investing. Even then, only a very small portion of your overall portfolio should be put at risk. If you win, it's great fun. If you lose, it's not.

WHAT ARE FUTURES AND OPTIONS?

Simply put, futures and options are contracts that allow you to buy or sell a specific commodity or security at a specific price within a certain period of time. The biggest difference between the two is that when you own a futures contract, you must carry out the transaction on a specified date. With an option, however, as the name indicates, you only carry out the transaction if you choose to. You also can do it anytime within a specified period, rather than on a specific date. If you don't exercise the option by the end of that period, the option expires.

Why buy either one? Some people buy them to protect themselves from losses on other investments. They're hedging their bets, and are therefore commonly known as hedgers. For example, futures contracts are often bought by companies that produce or consume commodities. Commodities are the raw materials we use every day of our lives—wheat, barley, sugar, meat, crude oil for gasoline and fuel oil, precious metals like silver, and thousands of other products. They are traded at exchanges around the country for cash in what's known as the spot market, since all purchases are paid for "on the spot."

The price of commodities follows the simple rules of supply and demand. Take wheat, for example. When wheat supplies are good, prices drop. But if bad weather should wreak havoc on the nation's wheat crop, supplies dwindle and prices shoot up. Similarly, when Middle East oil imports are unrestricted, the price of crude oil will remain stable or even fall a bit. But if suppliers slow the flow of oil, prices start to climb.

And it's not just the prices of the raw materials that go up. Products made from those materials also increase in price. When wheat prices go up, we pay more for flour and bread. When oil prices increase, gasoline and fuel oil prices rise.

People who buy commodities futures do so to protect themselves from drastic price shifts. If a baking company buys future contracts to buy wheat at $3.00 a bushel, it's protected if the price rises. In fact, many manufacturers who use vast quantities of raw materials will buy futures contracts to allow themselves to create a more concrete business plan. With the futures contracts in hand, they know what they'll pay for their raw materials, and price shifts are of less concern. Likewise, the producers of raw materials—loggers, farmers, and miners—will buy futures contracts to ensure they receive a certain amount for their products.

Options also can provide protection from losses. For example, let's go back to those 100 shares of the XYZ Corporation you purchased at $30 a share in chapter 4. Your investment risk is that the price of the stock will drop and you'll lose money. To protect yourself, you can buy an option to sell the stock for $30 a share within a certain period of time. You'll pay the seller of the option a premium, but if the stock should fall through the floor, it'll be worth every penny. You can exercise the option, get back your original investment, and limit your losses to the money you paid for the option.

FUTURES AND OPTIONS AS INVESTMENTS

For investors, the loss prevention quality of futures and options is of little interest. They see futures and options as high-risk investment strategies that can produce enormous profits (and equally enormous losses). That's why these people are called spéculators.

Such high-stakes gains (and losses) are possible because trading in futures and options is characterized by enormous leverage. This means that with a relatively small cash outlay, you can make an investment of much greater value. For example, a futures contract can usually be purchased for about 10 percent of its value. Options are also purchased for a fraction of the value of the underlying securities.

Making Money with Futures

To trade futures, investors enter an order to buy or sell a specific commodity at a certain price on a certain date. Let's say you enter a futures contract to buy September wheat for $3.00 a bushel. (All futures contracts expire on the third Friday of the specified month, so if you hold on to it, your order to buy wheat would be executed on the third Friday in September.) A single wheat contract is worth 5,000 bushels, so the contract would cost $15,000. But you're only required to pay 10 percent, or $1,500, for the contract. It's considered a good faith deposit and is called the initial margin.

But you have no intention of actually executing the contract. What are you going to do with 5,000 bushels of wheat? What you're doing is gambling that wheat prices—and therefore the value of your contract—will rise and you'll be able to get out of the deal with a tidy profit before the contract has to be executed.

Let's say that by the end of August wheat prices have risen to $3.30 a bushel. This means your contract is now worth $16,500. To cash in and collect your profit (which will be diluted by commissions and other costs, by the way), you cancel your obligation to buy wheat by entering a second contract to sell September wheat. (Conversely, if you originally enter a futures contract to sell a commodity, you enter a buy contract to get out of it.)

But what happens if wheat prices fall? Bad things, to be sure. Let's say that by late August, wheat prices have fallen to $2.70 a bushel. Your contract that was once worth $15,000 is now worth only $13,500. Your first problem is that if you want to ride the deal out over a longer period you'll have to add money to your original $1,500 investment to maintain your margin. To get out of the deal, you again enter a contract to sell September wheat and then retire to lick your wounds.

Sometimes people make money with futures simply because of circumstances. There's a legendary futures story about a group of television weathermen in Florida. Some years ago, a massive cold snap hit the Sunshine State. Being weathermen, they realized this was going to happen before the general public did and they pooled all their available resources and bought up every orange juice future they could lay their hands on. Of course, when the news became public, a lot of other people did the same thing. But the weathermen, with their advance knowledge, got there first and were able to buy in before prices began to rise.

Sure enough, a few days later Florida's temperatures did indeed plummet, and the state's orange growers suffered huge losses. As a result, the price of orange juice went through the roof, and the little conglomerate of weathermen investors made out very well indeed.

Making Money with Options

An option gives you the right (but not the obligation) to buy or sell a specified security for a certain price (called the strike price) within a designated period of time, usually five months or less. If the price of the underlying security—they can be stocks, Treasury bills or bonds, currency, stock or bond market indexes, and even futures—moves in the direction you hope it will, you make money. Options to buy securities are known as calls, and options to sell are called puts.

Option prices.

The price, or premium, paid for an option is determined by how far away the strike price is from the actual price of the security at the time you buy the option and how far away the option is from expiration. During the life of the option, its value is also affected by fluctuations in the price of the underlying security. When a security's value rises, calls also increase in value, while puts decrease. Conversely, when the price of a security decreases, puts increase in value and calls decrease. This fluctuation allows people to make money by simply buying and selling options. (This is the realm of professional option traders, however. It's not for people saving for college.)

Buying options.

People who buy calls are betting that the price of the underlying security will increase. For example, if you buy a call option to buy XYZ stock for $30 a share and the price increases to $34, you exercise the option, buy the stock at $30, and immediately sell it at $34. Your profit is $4 a share less the premium you paid for the option.

People who buy puts, on the other hand, are hoping for a decrease in the value of the underlying security. Let's say you buy a put option to sell XYZ stock at $30 a share and the price drops to $26. You buy the stock at $26 and immediately sell it for $30. Again, your profit is $4 a share less the cost of the option.

Selling options.

As an investor, you can also take the other side of the deal and be a seller, or writer, of options. The basic strategy behind selling options is to collect the premium and have the price of the underlying security move in such a direction that the buyer allows the option to expire. If the buyer decides to execute the option, however, you have the obligation to carry out the transaction.

It can be quite painful. Sellers of calls are either covered, meaning they actually own the security in question, or naked, meaning they don't (they're shorting the options, just like people short stocks). Both are extremely vulnerable to a big move in the price of the underlying security.

Let's say XYZ stock is trading at $30 a share and you sell a call option to sell it at $35. One option contract is equivalent to 100 shares of stock, so you're promising to sell the buyer of the call 100 shares of XYZ for $35 a share. You collect the premium and hope the price doesn't start to rise. As long as it stays below $35, the buyer won't exercise the option.

But to your horror, it takes off like a rocket and soon reaches $45 a share. At this point, the holder of the call understandably decides to exercise the option and make a lot of money. You, however, could be looking at trouble.

If you own the 100 shares, you're not in too bad a shape. You can either sell your stock to the buyer, losing potential profit, or buy a call to cancel your obligation and keep the stock. The latter is obviously the preferred strategy. Since the stock has risen in value so much, you'll want to hold on to it. But the call you have to buy to cover your obligation will wipe out the profit from the premium you received earlier.

If you're a naked seller of options, on the other hand, and don't own the stock, you're one of the biggest fools in the investment world. In this case, you have two choices. One, you can buy the 100 shares of XYZ on the market at $45 a share and sell them to the buyer for $35 a share to meet your obligation. In this case, you lose $1,000 less whatever you received as the premium. Or, two, you can buy a call to buy the stock at $35 a share (at an astronomical premium), exercise the option, and then turn right around and sell the stock at $35 to meet your obligation. In this case, you lose the difference between the two premiums. In both cases, you lose your shirt.

ARE FUTURES AND OPTIONS REALISTIC STRATEGIES?

Futures and options are complex, high-risk investment strategies, and this chapter has only skimmed the surface to give you a basic idea of how they work. If you're interested in them, can afford the risk, and don't mind doing some homework, they can be an intriguing way to invest some of your money.

Should you turn to brokers for advice? In my opinion, no. The majority of stockbrokers and financial planners know just enough about futures and options to get you in trouble. But that doesn't mean they won't help you invest your money. After all, as we learned earlier, they'll make a profit on the deal regardless of how you fare.

You really need to rely on yourself for this one. Do careful research, read as much as you can about futures and options, and seek out investors who have had experience with them. And don't invest until you're absolutely sure you know what you're doing and you're comfortable with the risk.

FOR MORE INFORMATION

Here are a few good books that will help you learn more about futures and options.

- *Options as a Strategic Investment* by Lawrence G. Macmillan, New York Institute of Finance, New York, 1993.
- *Options, Futures and Other Derivatives* by John Hull, Prentice-Hall, New York, 1997.
- *Understanding Options* by Robert W. Kolb, Wiley, New York, 1995.

WHAT'S NEXT?

It's time to turn away from Wall Street and look at some other ways to invest for your child's college education. One of the most popular investment strategies is to buy real estate rental properties. There are also retirement funds that can serve as sources of capital down the road. We also need to talk about life insurance. It's a lousy investment, but it is necessary to insure that the money for college will be there if you or your spouse should pass away. These are the topics of chapter 8.

8

REAL ESTATE, LIFE INSURANCE, AND RETIREMENT ACCOUNTS

In the previous few chapters, we looked at traditional investments such as stocks, bonds, and mutual funds. These are the most popular investments for people saving for college, but they're certainly not the only choices. This chapter looks at some other ways you can put your money to work.

REAL ESTATE

When you're considering investment strategies, don't forget real estate. For the homeowner, the appreciation in their property over the years builds equity that can be tapped to pay tuition down the road. People who invest in rental property enjoy a steady income that can be socked away in any of the investments we discussed in the previous chapters. They also can make money on the appreciation of the property while they own it. Some people make money by buying and rehabilitating run-down properties and then reselling them.

The first and most common strategy, of course, is to buy a home. It's still the traditional American dream. But before you do it, you need to ask yourself one very important question.

Are You Better Off Renting?

Conventional financial wisdom has always said buy a house, for the simple reason that it helps you build equity. It's kind of like a forced savings plan—send the check in every month or find yourself without a roof over your head.

But sometimes you have to ask yourself whether you can't save more money renting. Some people are able to find wonderful rental arrangements that allow them to sock away significant amounts of money every month.

I was once one of them. From 1978 to 1984 my wife and I rented a beautiful 200-year-old, three-story stone house in the very northeast corner of Maryland just a few miles from the Pennsylvania and Delaware state lines. The house has five fireplaces, a gorgeous spiral staircase, and sits on a 5,400 acre piece of property that had once been owned by a member of the DuPont family. In the early '70s the family sold the property to the State of Maryland, and it has since been managed by the state's Department of Natural Resources.

There are a half dozen such houses on the property and, rather than let them sit vacant and deteriorate, the state rents them out. Fortunately for us, nobody in the Department of Natural Resources paid much attention to rental market prices, and we paid $350 a month, including utilities, for the place. It was the deal of a lifetime.

During the six years we lived there (during which time the rent never changed), we were able to save enough money to amass a sizable down payment for the first home we purchased and also get a good start on our children's college accounts. Had we been shelling out $600 or $700 a month for a mortgage—almost all of which would have been to pay interest—plus utilities, maintenance costs, and property taxes, it's unlikely that we'd have been able to save very much at all. Any equity we would have built up during the same period would have been the few dollars in principal included in our mortgage payment each month and any appreciation in the value of our house.

Of course, like most people, we ended up buying a house when our careers took us to another state. And we did make some money when we sold it and bought our present house. But had we stayed where we were, as far as I'm concerned we'd still be living in our 18th-century stone mansion and socking $1,000 away in mutual funds every month.

Home Equity Loans

If you do make the plunge and buy a home, you're creating a pool of equity that can be tapped to help meet college expenses when they arrive. This can be done by taking out a home equity loan.

Home equity loans, which are really just second mortgages cloaked in a less threatening name, are quickly becoming one of the most popular forms of financing for all sorts of things, including college tuition. Banks like home equity loans because there is virtually no risk involved. If the borrower defaults on the loan, the bank has a very tangible asset—the borrower's home—to back up the loan.

Let's say your home is worth $150,000, and your mortgage balance is $50,000. That means you have $100,000 worth of equity in your home. You can borrow against that equity—usually up to 70 percent of its value—to help meet college costs. The downside, however, is obvious. You're putting your house on the line. If you can't keep up with the payments, you may suddenly find yourself without a roof over your head.

Approach your search for a home equity loan just like you did for your first mortgage. Call the commercial banks, credit unions, and savings and loans in your area to shop around for interest rates. Are they offering fixed-rate or variable-rate loans? If they're variable-rate, how is the rate adjusted, and what is the cap? Are there additional up-front fees you'll have to pay? Will you have to pay "points," a percentage of the principal (usually 1 to 3 percent), at the beginning of the loan? Remember to include any fees paid at the beginning of the loan to your total start-up costs.

Check with your accountant to see if you should get the kind of loan where you pay off some of the principal each month or the kind where you just pay off the interest each month and then pay back the principal in a giant "balloon" payment at the end of the loan. But remember, if you don't have the cash to make the last payment, you'll have to refinance.

Approach home equity loans with caution. They can be a great resource. They can also drag you into financial ruin. If you're like most people, your home is your most precious asset. If you're going to risk it to pay for college, do your homework very, very carefully to make sure you can cover the monthly payments.

Investing in Income Properties

Many people make money in real estate by purchasing property which they then rent. The income from the rent plus the appreciation on the value of the property can provide an excellent return on investment. There are several approaches.

Renting a portion of your home.

I live in a medium-sized town in upstate New York that has two colleges. One is a large, well-known Ivy League university with about 18,000 students, and the second is a smaller private college with about 5,000 students.

Because of the large student population and the nomadic nature of academics in general, the demand for rental units here is enormous. I know many people who own homes that include apartments they rent out. Often the apartment is a small wing of the house that was either part of the original floor plan or something some enterprising homeowner added later. Some are attic or basement units. Others are duplexes in which the owner occupies one side of the house, and renters occupy the other. The rental units have their own entrances, allowing both the renters and the homeowners to enjoy their privacy.

For the owners of these properties, the rent they receive covers part, if not all, of their mortgage payments and sometimes even their property and school taxes. In the meantime, they're squirreling away the equivalent in various investments to pay for college and retirement. All the property owners I know are convinced that buying a home with a rental unit was the smartest financial move they ever made.

Buying an income property.

Other people in town own single-family houses or multiunit apartment houses that they rent out to students. Since they don't live in the properties, the arrangement is purely an investment. They make money as long as the rental income they receive is more than the cost of owning the property. They also benefit from any appreciation in the properties themselves over time.

Other people own commercial properties that they rent out to small business owners. Again, as long as their rental income exceeds their costs, they make money.

Income properties are frequently excellent investments. But there are a few downsides that must be considered.

What are the costs of owning the property? Owning a rental property is not a one-way street. Sure, you'll have income from the rent the property generates, but you'll also be responsible for taxes, as well as the cost of maintaining the building and the grounds. The plumbing and electrical systems need to be kept in good repair, and the roof must be free of leaks. The heating system must be kept in good working order. Both the inside and outside of the building will need to be painted periodically. Carpeting and flooring will need maintenance and periodic replacement. In the summer, there's grass to mow. In the winter, sidewalks and driveways must be kept clear of snow and ice.

Crunch the numbers very carefully before you invest in an income property. You're getting involved in a business of sorts, and as with any business, you need to create a business plan. Figure out the costs of owning the property, and then do a realistic assessment of the income it will generate. If the profit is there, go for it. If it's not, don't kid yourself. Look for another property to buy.

Can you always fill the units? If you own a home with an attached apartment, a vacancy can be a hardship as far as cash flow is concerned, but you'll survive. You'll just have to pay your mortgage yourself until you find a new renter.

But if you own a separate single-family dwelling, a multiunit dwelling, or a commercial property, vacancies can end up costing you money. If you rely one hundred percent on the rental income to cover the costs associated with owning the property, any long-term vacancy will be very painful financially. You need to make sure you have the resources to survive such periods before you decide to invest in this type of property.

Can you find responsible tenants? An income property only earns money if you can collect the rent. Sometimes this can be a real problem. A friend of mine named Dave owns a small house here in town, and for the last couple of years he's been plagued with a succession of tenants from hell. The most recent one was an itinerant, burned-out refugee from the '60s who calls himself Star Child (like any good college town, we attract our share of weirdos).

Star Child was definitely one with the universe, but he didn't quite understand the concept of rent. When Dave went to the house to kick him out, the guy's response was, "Oh, man, I can't handle this," and he immediately sat on the floor in the lotus position and began to chant some sort of mantra. It finally took the threat of legal action to get him to leave (apparently he was familiar with the concept of arrest).

Real Estate Investment Trusts

If you're not interested in being a landlord, real estate investment trusts (REITs) are a slightly different twist on investing in real estate. In the last few years, they have become more and more popular with people looking for high-return investments that can weather downturns in the stock market.

REITs are companies that own, manage, and develop properties such as shopping malls, apartment complexes, and resorts. As of early 1997 there were around 300 publicly traded REITs with a combined market value of around $70 billion. At least a third of them have been created since 1993, and the largest have capitalization of more than $1 billion.

Although REITs are not completely new to the investment world, their performance in 1996 attracted a lot of attention as they outperformed the Standard & Poor's 500 by more than 50 percent, with a 36 percent return, as opposed to the S&P 500's 23 percent return. Two REITs, Patriot American Hospitality and Starwood Lodging, had gains of 75 percent and 92 percent, respectively.

Another characteristic of REITs that has investors swooning is their stability in a falling market. They showed this ability in the July 1996 downturn, and they also weathered the last quarter of 1987 fairly well. For those of you too young to remember, or for those of you with short memories, that quarter included the biggest one-day stock market crash in history.

REITs are also popular because of their high dividend yield (the annual dividend divided by the share price). Because they are required to distribute 95 percent of their net earnings to shareholders, yields can be 8 percent or more. Many investment analysts expect them to provide a total annual return of 13 to 15 percent over the next five years.

The downside of REITs is the fact that, since they are a relatively young industry, there are no benchmarks investors can use to measure performance. For this reason, they should represent only 5 to 10 percent of your total portfolio. Look carefully at the type of property the trust is involved in, the geographic market, and the experience of the trust's managers before you invest.

LIFE INSURANCE

I only bring up the subject of life insurance in this book for one reason—you need it to make sure the money is there for college if you or your spouse should pass away unexpectedly. I don't consider it a good investment for college, however, and that's why I recommend the following.

Buy Term Insurance Only

When you buy life insurance, you typically have two choices—cash value insurance or term insurance. With a cash value policy (this includes whole life insurance, universal life insurance, variable life insurance, and other flavors), part of your premium is invested by the insurance company, and you build equity in the policy over time—equity you can tap down the line for college. A term policy, on the other hand, does not build equity. It just guarantees that if you die, your beneficiaries will receive the face value of the policy and nothing else.

The insurance industry would have you believe that cash value life insurance is the greatest investment you can make for college. They'll point out that not only are you guaranteeing that the money for college will be there if you should pass away but you're also building a nest egg for your child's college fund.

Technically, this is true. You do build equity. The problem is you're paying many times what a term policy would cost, and very little of the difference between the two is actually being invested. Most of it ends up in the coffers of the insurance company and the pocket of the salesperson who sold you the policy (an insurance salesperson will make about ten times more commission for selling you a cash value policy than for a term policy). What that money should be doing is sitting in a retirement fund or a mutual fund with your name on it.

One of the arguments made in favor of cash value policies is that their premiums are "paid up" after a certain number of years. In other words, the policy continues to be in effect, but you won't be shelling out any more money. Meanwhile, a term policy's premiums have to be paid like clockwork as long as you own the policy.

Again, technically, this is sometimes true. But since the premiums for a cash value policy are so much higher than those for a term policy, the total outlay for the cash value policy will be much higher. All you're really doing is paying the premiums in advance (and look who ends up with the money). It would take another 20 to 30 years of term premiums to match what you'd pay for a cash value policy that's considered "paid up" after 15 or 20 years.

And don't be fooled by the concept of your policy being "paid up." If you live long enough, there's a good chance you'll eventually exhaust those prepaid premiums and suddenly get a letter from the insurance company saying you need to put more money into the policy if you want it to stay in effect.

Another argument for cash value policies is that term insurance premiums keep increasing as you age. Again, true. But very few people need life insurance after a certain point in their lives. Once the kids are educated and on their own, the house is paid off, and pensions, social security and retirement account income all kick in, life insurance becomes a big waste of money.

But perhaps the biggest problem with cash value life insurance is its cost. Because it's so expensive, most people are unable to afford the coverage they need. Nevertheless, buffaloed by the earnest pitch of the salesperson and convinced that they're doing the best thing for their children's future, they buy it anyway. So there they are, underinsured, paying huge premiums, and building equity at a snail's pace. If they took the same amount of money, bought a term policy, and invested the difference in a selection of mutual funds, they'd have the same amount of insurance coverage and a heck of a lot more money in their college fund.

Despite all this, at least 75 percent of the life insurance policies sold today are cash value policies. It just goes to show you how effective the industry's marketing efforts are. Don't be lured in. Term policies are the only way to go.

How Much Do You Need?

The main purpose of life insurance is to provide a chunk of cash that replaces the projected income of the person who has died. The insurance industry provides its customers with worksheets, most of which are overly complicated, to help them determine how much they need. There's really just one main question you need to ask yourself: What expenditures do I want to make sure are covered and how much money is needed to cover them?

The answer to this question will vary widely. A two-income couple who both make good salaries may decide that they each only need enough insurance to pay off the mortgage and cover a portion of their projected college costs. A couple in which only one person brings home an income may decide the breadwinner should be heavily insured, while the other partner needs only a small amount of insurance. People with more children will probably want more coverage than people with just one or two children.

You should also find out how much in Social Security survivors' benefits your spouse and children will qualify for if you should pass away. Benefits for the surviving spouse are tied to his or her income, but your children will qualify. You can contact the Social Security Administration at 800-772-1213 for information on survivors' benefits.

Beyond that, the individual financial situation of each family must be considered. How much money have they already put aside? What can they expect to receive from inheritances? Are there other sources of income they currently draw from or will draw from in the future?

Weigh your needs carefully to make sure you buy enough coverage. Also guard against buying too much coverage. Remember, insurance is a lousy investment no matter how you look at it.

Buying Term Life Insurance

You can buy life insurance through just about any insurance agent. You may also be able to buy it for a very competitive price through your employer, particularly if you work for a large corporation, a school or university, a state government, or the federal government. You can also call several insurance agency quotation services like SelectQuote (800-343-1985) and Direct Insurance Services (800-622-3699). These companies represent the highest-quality, lowest-cost companies available and will provide you with information over the phone. If you buy a policy from them, they receive a commission from the company that issues the policy.

There are two important questions to ask when you're shopping around for term insurance. (Speaking of shopping around, you should do just that. Term insurance varies in price from company to company, so make a few calls and get quotes. This will allow you to get an overall picture of what the market is like and help you compare policies.)

How often does the premium get adjusted? As we just learned, the premiums for term insurance increase as the years go by. This is for the simple reason that the older you get, the more likely you are to die, and the greater the insurance company's risk that it's going to have to pay out the value of the policy (believe me, if anyone has the concept of risk down to a science, it's insurance companies).

Term policies can increase annually or every 5, 10, 15, or 20 years. The longer the period between adjustments, the greater the price increase. The advantage to longer periods between adjustments is knowing what your expenses are going to be. On the other hand, you'll pay a bit more in the early years of the policy.

Does the insurance company guarantee renewal? This is an extremely important question. A renewable policy guarantees that the company cannot cancel the policy should you become ill. Do not buy a policy that does not have this guarantee.

RETIREMENT ACCOUNTS

Either through your employer, through your own initiative, or both, you more than likely have (or will have by the time your child is ready for college) a significant amount of money put aside in retirement accounts. These can be a source of money to help pay for college.

How Retirement Accounts Work

Retirement accounts allow you to put aside a certain amount of money each year. In most cases, the money earns interest without being taxed until you begin to withdraw it. You can also usually deduct the amount you contribute from your gross income so you pay less in income taxes each year. If you withdraw any money before you reach age 59½, you pay a penalty in addition to the taxes due.

What you can do before age 59½, however, is borrow from the account and then repay the account with interest. But in many cases the interest you pay goes back into the account, so you're really paying yourself for the use of your own money. Following are the most common form of retirement accounts.

401(k) plans are offered by for-profit companies to their employees. The maximum amount you're allowed to contribute changes every year (in 1996 it was $9,500). You can have the money deducted directly from your paycheck and deposited in your account. Some employers match their employees' contributions up to certain percentage of their salaries. Contributions to a 401(k) are deducted from your gross income and are not subject to state and federal income taxes.

403(b) plans are offered to the employees of nonprofit organizations. Like those of a 401(k), the contributions to a 403(b) are exempt from federal and state taxes. Employees are allowed to contribute $9,500 or 20 percent of their salary every year, whichever is less. Longtime employees of an organization may be allowed to contribute even more.

457 plans are also made available to the employees of nonprofit institutions. But they have a couple of significant differences from 403(b) plans. One, the limit for contributions is $7,500 a year. Two, contributions are not kept separate from the organization's funds, so if the organization runs into financial trouble (a very common problem for nonprofits, by the way) your savings could be jeopardized.

SEP-IRAs (Simplified Employee Pension Individual Retirement Accounts) allow you to put aside up to 13 percent of your salary each year, or a maximum of $22,500. Like other retirement accounts, you pay no federal or state income tax on your contributions.

Keogh plans allow you to put even more money away each year—as much as 20 percent of your income up to $30,000. If you establish a Keogh plan, you are committed to staying with your employer for a certain number of years in order to be vested in, or have a right to, the full value of the plan. You can choose from a variety of Keoghs, each of which has different contribution rates and different methods of contributing.

IRAs (Individual Retirement Accounts) are for anyone with employment income. The annual contribution limit is $2,000. If your spouse is not employed, he or she can put $250 annually into what's called a spousal IRA. Recipients of alimony can also contribute to an IRA.

The problem with IRAs is that you have to pay income taxes on your contributions unless your adjusted gross income is below a certain amount ($25,000 if you're single, $40,000 if you're married and file jointly) or the IRA is the only retirement plan in which you participate. (Under certain conditions, you may qualify for a partial IRA deduction.) Regardless of whether your IRA is taxed, however, the interest that compounds over the years remains untaxed until you begin to withdraw funds.

Because of the potential tax problem, you should only put retirement income in an IRA after you've made the maximum contributions to your other retirement plans.

What If You're an "Older" Parent?

Many people today are becoming parents in their forties and even their fifties. Some choose to wait to have children until they're financially secure. Others are remarrying after a divorce or the death of a spouse and starting all over again with a second set of children.

If you're one of these late bloomers, and you're 59½ or older with children entering or already in college, you can begin to withdraw the money in your retirement accounts without penalty. It's a perfect solution to the college tuition problem. (Of course, it may create problems for your retirement, but, hey, you're the one who got yourself into this situation.)

WHAT'S NEXT?

The investment decisions you make to pay for college will be determined by your income, current obligations, spending habits, tolerance for risk, and many other factors. But looming over them all will be time. Regardless of everything else, the number of years you have until you start writing those tuition checks will have the most influence on your investment strategies. In chapter 9, we'll look at some proven investment strategies and how those strategies will change as college draws closer.

9

TIME AND MONEY—INVESTMENT STRATEGIES THAT WORK

As we learned earlier, when it comes to investing wisely for college, there's one simple rule: The more time you have, the better off you'll be. If you start saving when your children are infants, the chances are excellent you'll have enough put aside by the time they reach college to cover your portion of the bills. But the longer you wait to begin to save, the greater the financial burden you'll face when they head off to school. If you're not careful, you may find yourself paying off loans well into your golden years.

As we also learned earlier, investment is accompanied by risk. But investment risk is mitigated by time. This means the longer you have to save, the more aggressive you can be in your saving strategies, particularly in the early years. As college gets closer, you can begin to diversify your portfolio into less risky investments. When it's just around the corner, you reduce risk even further. Here's how it's done.

HOW MUCH WILL YOU NEED?

The first step is to come up with a ballpark figure on just how much you're going to need. Here's a simple method to help you figure it out. It assumes a 7 percent annual increase in college costs and a 7 percent return on your investments. It also assumes your child will enter college at age 18 and that you'll continue to save until he or she graduates.

1. Current one-year cost __________
2. Four-year cost in current dollars (multiply line 1 times 4) __________
3. First year's investment (Multiply line 2 by the number corresponding with your child's age in column A.) __________
4. Amount to invest each subsequent year (Multiply the amount on line 3 by the number corresponding with your child's age in column B.) __________

Child's Age	*A*	*B*
Newborn	.060	1.04
1	.062	1.08
2	.065	1.13
3	.067	1.17
4	.070	1.22
5	.073	1.27
6	.077	1.32
7	.081	1.37
8	.085	1.42
9	.091	1.48
10	.097	1.54
11	.104	1.60
12	.113	1.67
13	.124	1.73
14	.138	1.80
15	.155	1.87
16	.179	1.95
17	.212	2.03

THE EARLY YEARS—GO FOR GROWTH

To do it right, you need to start saving when your child is an infant. (If you're really on the ball, you'll start before your children are even born.) This will provide you with the maximum amount of time needed to amass the considerable amount of money you're going to need 18 years down the road.

As a long-term investor, you can be aggressive and seek higher-risk growth investments. Begin with stocks. Although you're almost certain to experience some market ups and downs, the fact that you have the time to ride them out means that over the long haul you should come out on top. Over the years, the stock market has outperformed all other investment options. During the last 70 years, blue-chip stocks have returned an average of 10.2 percent a year, and small company stocks have returned an average of 12.4 percent. As this book was being written, the market was riding the crest of an unprecedented bull market that took the Dow Jones industrial average over the 8,000 level for the first time in history.

Should you buy stock in individual companies? Sure, if you've done careful research and don't mind the risk. But don't put more than 10 to 15 percent of your portfolio in individual stocks. Rather, buy stock mutual funds, which reduce risk. They offer professional management and expert research on promising companies. They also will automatically reinvest your dividends so your fund can grow with almost no effort on your part.

As I mentioned earlier, there are more than 6,000 mutual funds available, offering a wide variety of options for everyone from the speculative risk-taker to the risk-allergic conservative. Since you have time on your side, you should begin with funds designed for growth. Most investment experts recommend a mix of up to 75 percent domestic funds and 10 to 20 percent carefully selected international funds. To reduce your risk a bit, put the balance in a conservative bond fund or a hybrid fund.

This is where research plays such an important role. Refer back to chapter 6 when evaluating different funds. Make sure you ask the right questions, and carefully read the prospectus of any fund you're considering. You need to know what companies the fund invests in and what fees are charged. Study the fund's past performance, and check out the reputation of the fund managers(s). Understand the tax implications and reinvestment options.

Most experts suggest a mix of five or six mutual funds for diversity and risk protection. You probably won't have a lot of money to invest at the start, so begin with a domestic growth and income fund that invests in the stocks of mid- to large-size companies. These are designed to provide a safe return but also pursue growth. As you have more money to invest, add one or more aggressive growth funds, a very aggressive small cap fund, and a less risky international fund.

What about futures and options? It's up to you. As I mentioned earlier, if you can afford the risk and are willing to learn how these volatile investment vehicles really work, they can be an interesting and profitable way to go. But remember, you can lose your shirt, so don't invest any more than you can afford to lose.

How long should you continue this strategy? Again, you have time on your side, so you can continue to be an aggressive investor until your child reaches eight or nine. Then it will be time to make some adjustments.

The Long-term Planners

Brandon and Helen Winter are practical people who plan ahead. They began putting money aside for college the day they decided to have a child. Their son, Paul, is now three years old and already has a diversified college fund composed of mutual funds and a few individual stocks.

The Winters hope to have a minimum of $150,000 set aside for Paul's education when he enters college. They know they have time on their side, so they've decided to follow conventional investment wisdom and shoot for the moon while Paul is little. Since they both work, they've been able to set aside a good portion of their income every month for his college fund.

The Winters' first mutual fund investment was a relatively young small cap fund that invests in emerging technology companies. It's been a rocky road. The first year the fund returned about 12 percent, but the second year that dropped to 3 percent. Nevertheless, they are confident in the fund and intend to hold on to it.

The next two funds they invested in were less risky. One is a growth fund that returned 18 percent its first year. The second is a growth and income fund that returned almost 14 percent. In the interest of balancing their portfolio, they recently made a small investment in a fund that invests in intermediate-term bonds. They also own shares in two individual companies. One manufactures software systems designed to streamline university administration operations, and its stock is going through the roof; the Winters have almost doubled their investment in just a year and a half. The other is a small biotechnology company started by a college friend of Brandon's. Its stock is floundering.

The Winters have both become knowledgeable investors and scour the financial pages daily. They plan to continue to be aggressive stock mutual fund investors for the next few years. Then they'll embark on the next strategy.

THE MIDDLE YEARS—DIVERSIFY TO REDUCE RISK

As your child approaches junior high, your interest will begin to switch from pursuing growth to protecting the gains you've made over the previous years. You're going to be more concerned with generating predictable returns than speculative profits. This means it will be time to begin a gradual switch from growth funds to less risky hybrid funds, income funds, and bond funds.

This isn't to say you can't continue to pursue growth. You can. In fact, the ideal balance at this point is a 50/50 ratio between stock funds and bond funds. And it's perfectly reasonable to have at least one stock fund that's reaching for big returns. That's half the fun of investing.

You don't have to make big adjustments all at once. Beginning when your child enters fourth grade, move 10 to 15 percent of the money you have invested in stock funds into bond funds or hybrid funds every year. You should also put around 75 percent of any new investment money into bond funds or hybrid funds. By the time your child enters high school, you'll have achieved a roughly 50/50 balance.

When you begin to consider bond funds, refer back to chapter 6. As with stock mutual funds, there are many choices and many questions to ask. Make sure the funds you choose meet your needs and that you understand all the fees involved.

The Late Starters

Alan and Lori Chandler are like many of us. They didn't think too much about paying for college until their daughter, Sara, reached junior high. Then they began to worry.

Unlike the Winters, who started investing early and will have established a fairly sturdy college fund by the time their son enters junior high, the Chandlers had to start from scratch. Still, they have six years to put together a nest egg and, although they won't have everything covered, they can at least take a significant bite out of their college costs.

The first thing the Chandlers did was make some financial changes to improve their cash flow and free up more money for investment. They began by refinancing their house at a lower interest rate, a move that cut almost $100 off their monthly mortgage. They got rid of one of their two monthly car payments by selling one of their late model cars and buying a used car for their second vehicle. This saved them another $230 a month and left them with $2,000 in cash. They also instituted a strict budget that allows them to save an additional $200 each month.

Since they started so late, the Chandlers had to steer away from high-risk growth strategies in favor of investments that provide more predictable returns They immediately invested the $2,000 proceeds from the sale of the car in a hybrid fund that earned an 11 percent return the first year. And they are funneling approximately $500 a month into two bond funds and a conservative large cap stock fund. Using this strategy, they hope to have at least $50,000 set aside by the time Sara enters college. They know this won't cover all her costs, and they plan on relying on scholarships, financial aid, and loans to cover the balance.

THE FINAL YEARS—PROTECT YOUR PROFITS

Once college is on the horizon, it will be time to become even more conservative. You'll have very real costs staring you in the face, and you'll need to know exactly how much money you have to meet them. This means that daring, swashbuckling investor that existed when your child was an infant must be transformed into a conservative, penny-pinching skinflint.

By the time your child is a junior in high school, you should put any money you have left in growth funds into income funds that provide a predictable return. You won't earn as much with these investments, but you'll virtually eliminate the downside risk.

The balance of your assets should be kept in bond funds. Many experts recommend that most be moved into mid- and short-term U.S. Treasury funds. These provide the best protection if interest rates should start to rise

Another strategy is to begin to purchase zero-coupon bonds. You'll recall that you purchase these at a discount and don't receive any income until the bond matures. At that point, you get back the money you paid for the bond plus the interest in one lump sum. With proper planning, you can purchase a series of zeros that mature just as your child's tuition bills arrive every year.

Series EE savings bonds are another popular choice. These are sold for half their value at maturity, and the interest they earn is exempt from state and local taxes. You'll recall from chapter 5 that if you have a child in college and cash in EE bonds to pay tuition, you may not have to pay federal taxes, either (this also applies to tuition for you and your spouse). Once again, here are the conditions that must be met.

- The bonds must have been purchased after 1990.
- The bonds must be purchased in the parents' name, not in the child's name.
- Parents must be at least 24 years of age.
- The money from the bonds must be used the same year the bonds are redeemed, and all the money must be used for tuition. It cannot be used for room and board.
- Parents must meet income requirements. In 1996, the adjusted gross income for a married couple had to be $61,850 or less ($41,200 or less for a single parent) to take advantage of the tax break.

Once your child is in college, liquidity becomes important, so you should begin to divert money into certificates of deposit and money market funds. Make sure the money market funds have cash transfer and check writing options. These will be important in paying bills and getting money to your poor impoverished student.

The Panic Stricken

Ed and Sue Doolittle are in a bind. They've waited too long to begin a college investment program, and now they have just two years until their son, Robbie, enters college. Are they sunk? No, not completely. But they have certainly created a huge problems for themselves.

It would be nice to be able to say there's a magic plan for people like the Doolittles. Unfortunately, there isn't. They really have just one choice: to save as much as they can as fast as they can. The first thing they need to do is follow the lead of the Chandlers and streamline their financial lives to free up as much money as possible. This money can then be directed toward conservative bond funds and income funds. To try anything more risky would potentially only add to their woes.

Beyond that, the Doolittles can only hope they qualify for a lot of financial aid and that Robbie can win some scholarships. But guess what? Contrary to what you might think, there's a good chance they can. Read on to learn how it's done.

WHAT'S NEXT?

So far this book has discussed a variety of investment options and strategies to help you save for college. But there's a very important topic we've ignored so far—how to manage your assets and how to handle income from gifts, inheritances, and other sources.

There's a very important reason for this. If you're like most people, you'll only have enough money set aside to cover a portion of your child's college expense. The rest will come from a variety of sources, including grants and financial aid. For this reason, you need to position yourself and your child in such a way as to qualify for the highest amounts of aid possible. We'll look at these issues in Part 2.

PAYING THE BILLS

PART 2
OTHER RESOURCES

Now that we've covered the most popular investment vehicles for saving for college, it's time to look at how you can tap other sources to make up the difference between what you'll need to spend and what you can afford to spend.

Earlier in the book I pointed out that the average family today has to come up with about 60 percent of college costs out of pocket. The remaining 40 percent comes from scholarships, grants, low-interest loans, and other forms of financial assistance. You'll be amazed by how much money is out there. In 1996 alone, the federal government shelled out almost $40 billion in grants, work-study subsidies, and low-interest loans to college students. Individual colleges and universities, corporations, foundations, and the 50 states contributed another $13 billion or so.

Part 2 of this book looks at how you can tap into this huge chunk of cash. We'll examine the financial aid process, the many federal and state programs that provide financial assistance to students, special funding sources for women and minorities, and alternative sources of assistance. We'll also look at athletic scholarships, prepaid tuition programs and other strategies to cut costs, and some of the ways your child can help foot the bill (now there's a concept).

But before we begin to look at sources of financial aid we need to look at how you can manage your assets to qualify for as much assistance as possible. This is because colleges, the federal government, and other financial aid providers have strict guidelines that govern the way they assess your need and ability to pay.

Your job is to paint a financial portrait of yourself that meshes with those guidelines and puts you as deep into the needy category as possible. You can accomplish this with the proper allocation of your assets.

10

THE FINANCIAL AID GAME—MANAGING YOUR ASSETS

Unless you are absolutely filthy rich, you should apply for financial aid. What's the worst thing that can happen? You'll be turned down. But you might be surprised, too. Many people who at first glance may seem unlikely candidates for financial aid actually end up qualifying for grants or subsidized, low-interest loans. The reason? They've steered their money into assets and accounts that are not considered by the government when it evaluates ability to pay.

There's another good reason to apply for financial aid. Even if you are turned down, the fact that you applied will make you eligible for loans that are not based on need.

THE BIG QUESTION—WHERE'S THE MONEY?

When you apply for financial aid, the federal government, state governments, colleges and universities, and other sources of assistance want to know as much as possible about your financial situation and your child's financial situation. Although they're ready and willing to provide financial assistance, they don't want to give it to people who don't need it.

Your first contact in the financial aid game will be the federal government when you fill out the Free Application for Federal Student Aid (FAFSA). This form is the starting point for everyone who applies for federal, state, or school financial aid.

The information you provide on your application form is run through a financial needs analysis by one of the financial aid services used by the government. They use a standard accounting procedure approved by the U.S. Congress. It considers your amount and sources of income, your assets, your age and need for retirement income, the number of other dependents you have, the number of kids you have in college, and many other financial factors. From this information, a determination is made on how much you should be able to pay, how much your child can pay, and how much financial aid you should receive.

WHO PAYS WHAT?

Currently, the federal government expects you to contribute around 6 percent of your assets each year to meet college costs. They expect this money to come from income, investments, and loans. Your child, however, is expected to contribute 35 percent of her assets plus a portion of her income.

This is because the government looks at your assets and your child's assets differently. Since your child theoretically has fewer financial commitments than you do (we'll assume she doesn't own a home, have children, or carry other big financial responsibilities), the government will expect a larger percentage of her assets to be used to pay for college. You, on the other hand, burdened as you are with a mortgage and all the other costs associated with raising a family, are expected to contribute much less. It's really quite reasonable.

HOW DOES THE GOVERNMENT ASSESS YOUR WEALTH?

This is where the process gets interesting—learning what the government considers and what it ignores when assessing your ability to pay. It doesn't take a genius to figure out that the poorer you are, at least on paper, the more financial aid you'll qualify for. So by shuffling assets around in a strategic—and thoroughly legal—manner, you can put yourself in a position to qualify for more financial aid. You're not trying to beat the system. You're just playing by the rules to maximize your advantage.

WHAT ASSETS DO THEY CONSIDER?

Here are the assets the government considers when evaluating your contribution to your child's college costs.

Income

They begin with your income from employment, rental property, Social Security, business ownership, and all other sources. This is all considered as a resource you can use to pay for college.

Checking Accounts, Savings Accounts, and Investments

These assets are also taken into account when assessing your ability to pay. They include cash, checking accounts, money markets, certificates of deposit, stocks, bonds, mutual funds, and any other investments.

Real Estate (Other Than Your Principal Residence)

If you own a vacation home, rental property, office building, land, or any other type of real estate, the government will consider that as an asset that can be counted in determining need.

Businesses

If you own a business, the government considers the value of the business as an asset.

WHAT ASSETS DO THEY IGNORE?

Here's the good news. There are two significant areas of equity that the government doesn't consider when assessing your financial aid needs. They both are excellent places to put money to reduce your assets on paper.

Retirement Accounts

Under the current financial aid system, money in retirement accounts is not considered when assessing need. This means you can have a million dollars in 401(k)s, IRAs, Keoghs, and other retirement accounts, but as far as the financial aid people are concerned, that money cannot be earmarked to pay for college. It's to keep you housed and fed when you're old and gray.

Is there a lesson to be learned here? You bet there is. One of the biggest mistakes you can make in saving for college is ignoring tax-free retirement accounts and putting all your money into taxable investments. Let's examine why.

First of all, when you put money into a retirement account, it's deducted from your gross income for the year, and you pay no income tax on that money until you begin to withdraw it after age 59½. Nor do you pay income tax on the interest the money accrues over the years. Money put into a non-retirement account, on the other hand, is subject to income taxes, as is the income the account generates. If you put the same amount of money into both a retirement and non-retirement account each month from the time your child is born, and they earn comparable interest rates, the value of the retirement account will be much higher by the time your child turns 18.

As we just learned, another reason to heavily fund your retirement accounts is that it qualifies you for more financial aid. Let's say you've socked away $100,000 by the time your child is ready for college. The greater the percentage you have in retirement accounts and the less in investments like mutual funds and bonds, the more needy you'll appear, at least on paper, and the more financial aid you'll receive

Finally, your retirement accounts are a source of funds from which you can borrow to pay for college. And when you do, you're borrowing the money from yourself, so your interest payments on the loans go right back into your own accounts. It's a win-win situation with three big "ifs." If you can't keep up with the repayment schedule, your loan to yourself will suddenly be considered a withdrawal and you'll have to pay income taxes on it. If you're younger than 59½, you'll also be assessed a penalty. And if you leave your employer for a new job, the borrowed amount will come due immediately.

Home Equity

The federal government also ignores equity in your home when evaluating need. This means you can reduce your paper net worth by paying off a considerable chunk of your mortgage or even your entire mortgage. Then, if you need money while your child is in school, you can tap into the value of your home with a home equity loan. And the interest on the loan is tax-deductible.

HOW DO COLLEGES LOOK AT ASSETS?

Unfortunately, many colleges are not quite as generous when it comes to assessing your financial need. In their formulas, they may include your home equity and your retirement accounts as assets. Check as early as possible with the financial aid offices of the college your child is considering to find out how they treat these two forms of equity in their own financial aid calculations.

WHOSE NAME(S) SHOULD GO ON YOUR ACCOUNTS?

If you plan on applying for financial aid, remember that the government expects your child to use 35 percent of her assets to help pay for college but only expects you to use 6 percent of yours. That makes the above question a no-brainer. Don't put your kids' names on the accounts. Keep them poor. They're not supposed to have money anyway.

THE IMPORTANCE OF TIMING YOUR INCOME

Financial aid is based on your financial history from the previous tax year, so anything you can do to reduce income for that year is to your advantage. Defer payment of income owed. Plan for the distribution of investment income or from the sale of real estate so that it doesn't fall in the year you'll be using on your financial aid applications.

MANAGING INHERITANCES AND OTHER WINDFALLS

I have some close friends—we'll call them Jim and Susan—who have a daughter who's a sophomore in college and a son who's a sophomore in high school. Needles to say, college costs are very much on their minds.

A few years ago Susan's mother passed away. She was a widow, and Susan was her only child and the sole beneficiary of her estate. She was not a wealthy woman. She lived comfortably on her husband's pension and Social Security but had little cash set aside and few investments. Her biggest asset was her house, which Jim and Susan sold for $145,000. She had around $35,000 in cash and securities. She also had a six-year-old Plymouth, which they sold for $4,500. After they sorted out her furnishings and belongings and decided what they wanted to keep, they sold the rest at auction and made another $8,000. After settling the estate and paying taxes and legal fees, they were left with about $110,000.

Jim and Susan are just two of the thousands or even millions of people who have large sums of money descend upon them. Some receive money through unexpected investment success, some exercise stock options, some enjoy great success in business, and a few even win the lottery. For most, however, the source is money and property left to them by parents or other relatives. In fact, the baby boom generation will be the recipient of more inherited wealth than any other generation in history.

For people saving for college, the arrival of such a windfall is obviously good news. For Jim and Susan, it means their daughter's college costs are completely covered and their son's are at least partially taken care of. But for many people, managing the money presents difficulties they're not always prepared to handle. Here are a few strategies everyone should follow.

Don't Rush into Any Decisions

You're experiencing what for most people is a once in a lifetime event. Take the time to educate yourself on investment strategies, and slowly put an investment plan together. In the meantime, either leave the money where it is or put it in short-term certificates of deposit or a high-yield money market fund.

Be Prepared for Sudden Popularity

It's also important to know that if word gets out about your sudden good fortune, you'll be besieged by calls and letters from stockbrokers and financial planners. Ignore them. Your financial windfall is to them the opportunity to sell you all sorts of investment products and earn nice commissions. If an investment adviser has the time to go fishing for new clients, it's a sign he had too much time on his hands. If he's good, people will be coming to him.

Pay Down Your Debt

If you have a lot of debt, particularly from high-interest credit cards, take the opportunity to pay at least some of it off. You'll be freeing yourself of annoying monthly payments, and you can redirect the same dollars to investments rather than bills.

Depending on the size of your windfall, you might even want

to pay off your mortgage. This makes particular sense if you still have quite a few years to save for college. By investing the money you were paying in mortgage costs and interest every month, you can quickly put together a very nice portfolio of investments. Plus, since colleges don't consider the equity you have in your home when evaluating you for financial aid, it's an excellent place to park your money. If you're lucky enough to live in an area where real estate is appreciating, it's even better. Down the road, should you need the money, the equity you have in your home can be a source of funds to help pay for college.

Diversify

When you do begin to invest, remember what we talked about in this chapter and earlier in the book. Risk is reduced by diversification. Direct your money to a variety of investments representing a variety of risk.

MONITOR CHANGES IN THE REGULATIONS

The government's financial aid regulations are constantly changing. What worked for you this year might not work next year. At the same time there may be some new wrinkles that can save you some money. Keep up with changes, and make sure you understand how they affect you.

BE HONEST!

As with your income tax returns, it's tempting to fudge the numbers a bit when dealing with financial aid forms. Don't do it. If you get caught, the penalties can be severe. It's not worth the few hundred dollars you might save yourself.

WHAT'S NEXT?

Now that you've learned how to maximize your chances for financial aid, it's time to look at the process itself. It's time consuming, confusing, and annoying. But it opens the gates to the more than $50 billion that's available in grants, scholarships, and low-interest loans every year. In chapter 11, we'll look at how you can tap into it.

11

THE FINANCIAL AID GAME—FINDING THE MONEY

In 1996, more than 60 percent of the students enrolled in America's colleges and universities received some form of financial aid. About 75 percent of the financial assistance came from the federal government. The rest came from the states, individual schools, corporations, foundations, and other sources.

If there's one rule that applies to financial aid, it's this: *Apply for every kind of financial aid you can think of, no matter how much money you make.* There are tens of thousands of sources of grants, scholarships, low-interest loan programs, work-study programs, and other kinds of financial aid out there. You just may find that you fall within the eligibility guidelines of some of them.

It's also important to be persistent. If you get turned down one year by a specific financial aid program, apply again the next year. If that doesn't work out, do it again the year after that. All it takes is time and some postage.

START EARLY

Playing the financial aid game properly requires time and should be started while your child is a freshman or sophomore in high school. As you'll learn later in this chapter, there are common procedures followed by everyone who applies for financial aid. But those will only lead you to the most common sources of assistance, like the big federal and state programs. To find the more obscure funding sources—those that may be offered by corporations, foundations, or other organizations—you'll need to do your own research, and that takes time.

WHAT DOES FINANCIAL AID PAY FOR?

Financial aid is designed to make up the difference between what a student and his or her parents can pay and the actual costs of college. As you would expect, it can be applied to tuition, fees, books, and other academic expenses. But what a lot of people don't realize is that it can also cover living costs like housing, food, and transportation. Also, not all financial assistance is designed for undergraduates in four-year programs. There are programs for graduate and doctoral students, as well as students attending vocational and trade schools.

HOW IS FINANCIAL AID AWARDED?

Financial aid comes in many forms and from many different sources. The most desirable are grants and scholarships. These are gifts, really, because the money does not have to be paid back.

Grants are almost always based on financial need. If they're federal or state grants, they're provided by tax dollars. Scholarships, on the other hand, are usually awarded by colleges, universities, corporations, private foundations, and other organizations. If they come from schools, they're usually from money generated by endowment. They differ from grants in that they're usually given as a reward for academic or societal or athletic achievement. (Those of you with 6'6" point guards who can run the break and play some D will become very familiar with scholarships. Lucky you.)

Other forms of financial aid include government-provided low-interest loans and work-study programs in which the student works a certain number of hours a week at a campus-based job.

Most students who apply for financial aid are offered a combination of all these types of assistance. The awards are "packaged" by college financial aid officers in an amount sufficient to cover that portion of the costs that parents and student cannot afford.

HOW AND WHEN SHOULD YOU APPLY FOR FINANCIAL AID?

The amount of money available for financial aid has been declining in recent years while college costs have been increasing. And of the dollars that are available, the amount steered toward grants and scholarships has been declining in favor of low-interest loans. The reason? Grants and scholarships don't have to be paid back. Loans do. This squeeze has served to make competition for financial aid tougher than ever, so it's important to start early. You're also dealing with the federal government and other bureaucracies, which takes time. Here's how the process works.

Filling Out the Application

Applications for financial aid should be filled out and submitted as early as possible during the second half of the senior year in high school. By January you should have all the forms you need, whether from your child's college or university or the high school guidance office. Everyone applying for financial aid of any kind must first file the Free Application for Federal Student Aid (FAFSA), so make sure you have a copy. Check with your child's college or university to find out if you'll need other forms for state or school programs. The deadline for filing applications is May 1 for the school year beginning the following fall. *Do not wait that long.*

Next, you and your child will have to gather the documents needed to complete the application forms. These include income tax returns, mortgage information, bank statements, business records, statements from investment and retirement accounts, and any other records pertaining to both your financial situations. Be extremely careful and deliberate in filling out the applications. Mistakes will slow up the process.

Mailing the Application

When you've completed the FAFSA application, mail it to: Application for Federal Student Aid, Federal Student Aid Programs, c/o FAFSA Processor, P.O. Box 6376, Princeton, NJ 08541-6376, or to Federal Student Aid Programs, c/o FAFSA Processor, P.O. Box 4032, Iowa City, IA 52243. If your school needs additional financial data, you can use the Financial Aid Form available from the College Scholarship Service, P.O. Box

6306, Princeton, NJ 08541-6306. Call 609-951-1025. These are services that specialize in evaluating financial need.

Confirmation Report

About three weeks after you send in your application, you'll receive a Confirmation Report. This allows you to review the information you submitted and make any corrections.

Notification of Eligibility

Two or three weeks later you'll receive a report detailing your family's expected contribution and your child's eligibility for financial assistance. The report will also go to your child's college or university and the appropriate state scholarship agency. If you've applied for a Pell Grant, you'll receive a Student Aid Report (SAR) indicating eligibility. You'll then send a copy of this to your child's college.

Notification of Aid

Most schools make financial aid decisions and send out letters notifying recipients between April and July. Your letter will tell you how much financial aid your child will receive for the school year, and it will break the figure down by source. These include federal sources of aid, such as Pell Grants, Supplemental Educational Opportunity Grants, Work-Study Programs, and Stafford and Perkins Loans; sources of aid from the college or university; state financial aid; and outside sources of aid.

The letter will also stipulate how grant and scholarship funds will be distributed and whether there are any special conditions attached. The interest rate and repayment conditions for loans will be described. It will also describe the type of work-study program your child will take part in, if applicable.

Accepting Aid

If you agree to accept the financial package you're offered, you and your child will sign and return a copy of the letter to the child's college or university. If you need additional money or have other questions, contact the financial aid office at the school immediately. Most schools have an appeals process that allows you to make your case for additional assistance.

Important Rules to Follow

The financial aid process is time consuming and often confusing and nerve-wracking. It's also extremely important. So it's critical that you take the time to understand it and follow the rules. Here are the most important.

Apply, no matter your income.

No matter your expectations. Everyone should apply for financial aid. If you get turned down, try again next year. If you get spurned again, apply the following year.

Apply early.

There's a lot of money out there, but it's not an infinite amount. If you wait too long to apply, you may miss the boat. Check deadlines and make sure your applications are in well ahead of them.

Register for the draft.

Register for the draft?!? Yes, male students have to be registered with the selective service to be eligible for federal assistance. Sorry I had to be the one to tell you.

Follow directions.

Financial aid applications can be mind boggling. Go slowly and follow directions. If the form says "please print," then print. If it asks you to use a pen, then use a pen. If it asks you to use a No. 2 pencil, use a No. 2 pencil.

Be neat.

Don't write in the margins or attach sticky notes. The neater your application, the more quickly it will be processed.

Make sure your applications are complete.

Double and triple check that you haven't left out any information. And whatever you do, don't forget to sign them.

Make copies.

Keep a copy of every financial aid form you submit.

Send the originals.

Only original application forms will be accepted.

Include your payment.

Don't forget to send a check, when required.

FINANCIAL AID TERMINOLOGY

Like most bureaucratic processes, the financial aid process has its own lingo, including the expected number of acronyms. Here are some of the most common.

•College Scholarship Service (CSS)—The CSS is an agency that analyzes financial need.

•Expected Family Contribution (EFC)—This is the amount you should be able to contribute for your child's college expenses. The number is determined by a formula established by Congress and is used to consider eligibility for a variety of federal loans.

•Free Application for Federal Student Aid (FAFSA)—This is the federal government's free application form, which must be filed for consideration for all Title IV federal financial assistance programs.

It's also used to determine eligibility for all federal student loans. Separate forms are usually needed for applications for state and college financial assistance programs.

•Financial Aid Form (FAF)—This is a form used to determine a family's financial need and ability to pay. The College Scholarship Service (CSS) processes these forms and sends the results to colleges and universities.

FAFs are used only when a student wishes to apply for non–Title IV funds or if a college requires supplemental data on a student.

•Simplified Needs Test—This financial aid application is used by families who have adjusted gross incomes under $50,000 and who file IRS Form 1040A or 1040EZ, or who don't have to file income tax returns.

•Student Aid Report (SAR)—This is the official notification of federal Pell Grant eligibility (or ineligibility). SARs usually arrive four to six weeks after applications are submitted and indicate the expected family contribution.

The three-part forms (two-part if a student is deemed ineligible) are then forwarded by the student to the appropriate colleges and universities, which then determine the amount of the Pell Grant. Ineligible students must forward their SARs to the appropriate schools in order to qualify for other types of financial assistance. Call 1-800-4-FED AID for information on Pell Grants.

WATCH OUT FOR FINANCIAL AID SCAMS

As with any valuable commodity, the demand for college scholarships has given birth to a number of scams. Most are run by companies that guarantee they'll find your child a grant or scholarship. In return, all you have to do is pay a modest fee.

This is exactly what happened to the parents of Andrew Brusker, a former high school football star from Pottstown, Pennsylvania. A talented running back with the size and speed that makes coaches drool, Andrew was being heavily recruited by a half dozen of the nation's most prestigious Division I college programs. Then the unthinkable happened. Early in his senior season he suffered a career-ending knee injury. All his hopes of a college scholarship ended with it.

Andrew and his parents were desperate. With three other children to put through college, they had been counting on the full scholarship the college scouts had assured Andrew he would receive. Without it, they weren't sure they could afford anything more than their local junior college. Then they were contacted by a company that guaranteed to find Andrew a grant or scholarship. The company's fee was $149.

The Bruskers paid the money and then waited. About two months later they received a list of about 50 scholarship and grant opportunities, loan programs, and competitions. Few of them were worth the effort it would take to fill out the application forms. The deadlines for some had already passed.

The company that conned the Bruskers was one of a half dozen scholarship search services that were charged with consumer fraud by the Federal Trade Commission in 1996. Collectively, the six companies were accused of bilking families out of more than $10 million. It's a practice that has increased as college expenses have continued to rise. According to the National Association of Student Financial Aid Administrators, an estimated 300,000 people were conned by scholarship search companies in 1996.

What should you look for when investigating the legitimacy of a company? Here are the three most common promises the con artists will make.

• They'll claim to have access to information that no one else has. In fact, the same information can easily be found with a little research in high school guidance offices, in libraries, and on the Internet.

• They'll promise to fill out and send in applications and do other tasks for you. This rarely happens.

• They'll guarantee to get your child a grant or scholarship. This is impossible. There are no guarantees with grants and scholarships.

It's important to note that there are legitimate scholarship search firms out there. But they're really just going to do work you could do yourself. A little time with reference books in libraries and on the World Wide Web will give you the same information they're going to sell you. There's really no reason to not do it yourself.

FEDERAL FINANCIAL AID PROGRAMS

The federal government has always shouldered the majority of the costs of providing financial aid to America's college students. In fact, colleges require students to apply to federal programs before they'll consider them for any other type of financial assistance. You can certainly understand this. They'd rather not give you any of their limited financial aid money if you're able to coax some out of the much deeper pockets of the federal government.

Historically, the government has been exceedingly generous in providing money for higher education. In recent years, however, budget cuts have reduced the amount of money available for grants and loans. In the mid-eighties, federal dollars accounted for about 84 percent of financial assistance for students. Today they make up about 75 percent of assistance.

The form of financial aid packages is changing, too. Ten years ago, a typical financial aid package consisted of about 80 percent grants, 17 percent loans, and 3 percent student employment. Today those numbers are about 46 percent, 50 percent, and 4 percent, respectively. In other words, the government now wants half the money it devotes to student assistance back, with interest. As a result, more and more students are graduating from college with substantial debt hanging over their heads (see the story of one financial aid recipient at the end of this chapter).

You must apply to federal financial aid programs every year, regardless of whether your child is already receiving assistance. And the rules for eligibility may change, in turn reducing (or increasing) the amount of aid your child might receive. However, the general rules for eligibility are: students must have a high school diploma or have earned a general equivalency diploma (GED), be enrolled as a regular student in an eligible school, be a U.S. citizen or eligible noncitizen, have a Social Security number, make satisfactory academic progress, and be registered with the selective service (males only).

Here are the major sources of federal financial aid.

Pell Grants

The Pell Grant Program is the government's largest need-based federal financial aid program. It's so broad, in fact, that students must apply for a Pell Grant before they can be considered for any other type of federal financial assistance. When putting together financial aid packages, college financial aid officers often use the Pell Grant as the foundation upon which the package is put together. The amount received is based on need and can be as much as $2,300 a year.

To qualify for a Pell Grant, students must meet the following criteria:

- They must demonstrate financial need.
- They must have a high school diploma or GED.
- They must be enrolled in or accepted by an approved school in either an undergraduate program or a certificate program.
- They must attend school at least half-time.
- They must maintain satisfactory academic progress.
- They must be free of any grant debt and not be in default of any loans.
- They must be U.S. citizens or eligible noncitizens.
- Males must be between 18 and 26 and have registered with the selective service.

- They must file a Statement of Educational Purpose guaranteeing that any money they receive will be used solely for educational purposes.
- They must sign an Anti-drug Abuse Act Certification.
- They must be working toward their first bachelor's degree. Students working on subsequent bachelor's degrees are not eligible.

Students should apply for Pell Grants after January 1 of their senior year in high school (or the January 1 before their planned attendance). The deadline for application is May 1. Call 800-433-3242 for more information on Pell Grants.

Supplemental Educational Opportunity Grants (SEOG)

SEOGs are supplemental to Pell Grants and are awarded to students with exceptional financial need; most come from families whose annual income is below $10,000. Priority is given to students who have already received Pell Grants. SEOGs can be as high as $4,000 a year. Extra money may be available if a student is enrolled in a study abroad program.

Each school that participates in the SEOG Program receives money from the government each year and then allocates the money through its financial aid office. SEOG funds are limited, and many students apply for these grants, so it's extremely important to apply early.

The qualifications for an SEOG are basically the same as those for a Pell Grant, with two exceptions. An applicant must have already applied for a Pell Grant, and he or she must demonstrate exceptional financial need.

Stafford Loans

The Stafford Loan Program provides low-interest loans to qualified students. The interest rate varies and is tied to the three-month Treasury bill rate, plus 3.1 percent. It's capped at 8.25 percent. There is no federal allocation dictating limits on the amount to be loaned, so everyone who qualifies for a loan gets one. Both undergraduate and graduate students are eligible for Stafford Loans, as are students enrolled in vocational programs and business, technical, and trade schools. In 1996, more than 3 million students borrowed money through the program.

Eligibility for Stafford Loans is determined by the financial aid officer of each school after reviewing the financial information of the applicant and the applicant's parents. Borrowing limits are $2,625 for freshmen, $3,500 for sophomores, and $5,500 for juniors and seniors. The total four-year borrowing limit for undergraduates is $23,000. Graduate and professional students also qualify for Stafford Loans and can borrow up to $8,500 each year.

About 70 percent of Stafford Loans are issued through banks, credit unions, and savings and loan associations. These financial institutions participate in the program for several reasons. The loans are insured by the federal government, and the government pays the interest on the loans while the borrowers are in school. The government also pays the lender a special fee that's tied to the interest rate on U.S. Treasury bills.

The remaining 30 percent are issued by colleges and universities participating in the Federal Direct Student Loan Program. In this case the lender is the U.S. Department of Education. Because all the paperwork is handled right at the school, these loans are usually less of a hassle to deal with.

Repayment of the principal and interest on Stafford Loans begins after a student has stopped attending college, regardless of whether he or she has graduated. There is a six-month grace period. Borrowers have up to 10 years to repay their loans, and the minimum monthly payment is $50, or $600 per year. There are certain situations in which repayment can be deferred. There are even some situations in which a loan may be forgiven. Most are those made to teachers, nurses, and other people working on behalf of communities or people in need.

Eligibility for a Stafford Loan is basically the same as that for a Pell Grant. Recipients must have their Pell Grant eligibility confirmed. For more information on Stafford Loans, contact the following guaranty agency in your state.

Alabama
Alabama Commission on Higher Education
1 Court Square, Suite 221
Montgomery, AL 36197-0001
205-269-2700

Alaska
Alaska Commission on Post Secondary Education
400 Willoughby Ave.
Pouch FB
Juneau, AK 99811
901-465-2962

Arizona
Arizona Educational Loan Program
2600 N. Central Ave., Suite 621
Phoenix, AZ 85004
800-352-3033 (in-state)
602-252-5793

Arkansas
Student Loan Guarantee Foundation of Arkansas
219 S. Victory
Little Rock, AR 72201
501-372-1491

California
California Student Aid Commission
P.O. Box 945625
Sacramento, CA 94245
916-322-0435

Colorado
Colorado Student Loan Program
999 18th St., #425
Denver, CO 80202
303-294-5050

Connecticut
Connecticut Student Loan Foundation
P.O. Box 1009
Rocky Hill, CT 06067
203-257-4001

Delaware
Delaware Post Secondary Education Committee
Carvel State Office Building
820 N. French St., 4th Floor
Wilmington, DE 19801
302-571-3240

District of Columbia
Higher Education Loan Program
1023 High St., N.W., Suite 100
Washington, DC 20005
202-289-4500

Florida
Office of Student Financial Assistance
Department of Education
Knott Building
Tallahassee, FL 32399
904-488-4095

Georgia
Georgia Student Finance Commission
2082 E. Exchange Pl., Suite 200
Tucker, GA 30084
404-493-5472

Hawaii
Hawaii Education Loan Program
P.O. Box 22187
Honolulu, HI 96822
808-536-3731

Idaho
Student Loan Fund Processing Center
P.O. Box 730
Fruitland, ID 83619
208-452-4058

Illinois
Illinois State Scholarship Commission
106 Wilmot Rd.
Deerfield, IL 60015
708-948-8550

Indiana
State Student Assistance Commission of Indiana
964 N. Pennsylvania St.
Indianapolis, IN 46204
317-232-2366

Iowa
Iowa College Aid Commission
201 Jewett Building
9th and Grand
Des Moines, IA 50309
515-281-4890

Kansas
Higher Education Assistance Foundation
6800 College Blvd., Suite 600
Overland Park, KS 66211
913-345-1300

Kentucky
Kentucky Higher Education Assistance Authority
1050 U.S. 127 South, Suite 102
West Frankfort, KY 40601
502-564-7990

Louisiana
Governor's Special Commission on Education and Services
P.O. Box 91202
Baton Rouge, LA 70821-9202
504-922-1011

Maine
Maine Education Assistance Division
Division of Higher Education Services
State House Station 119
Augusta, ME 04333
207-289-2183

Maryland
Maryland Higher Education Loan Corporation
2100 Guilford Ave., Room 305
Baltimore, MD 21218
410-333-6555

Massachusetts
Massachusetts Higher Education Assistance Corporation
Berkeley Place
330 Stuart St.
Boston, MA 02116
617-426-9796

Michigan
Michigan Higher Education Assistance Authority
Box 30047
Lansing, MI 48909
517-373-0760

Minnesota
Higher Education Assistance Foundation
85 E. Seventh St., Suite 500
St. Paul, MN 55101
612-227-7661

Mississippi
Mississippi Guarantee Student Loan Agency
3825 Ridgewood Rd.
P.O. Box 342
Jackson, MS 39211-6453
601-982-6663

Missouri
Coordinating Board for Higher Education
P.O. Box 1438
Jefferson City, MO 65102
314-751-3940

Montana
Montana Guaranteed Student Loan Program
33 S. Last Chance Gulch
Helena, MT 59620
406-444-6594

Nebraska
Higher Education Assistance Foundation
Cornhusker Bank Building
Suite 304
11th & Cornhusker Hwy.
Lincoln, NE 68521
402-476-9129

Nevada
Nevada State Department of Education
400 W. King St.
Capitol Complex
Carson City, NV 89710
702-885-5914

New Hampshire
New Hampshire Higher Education Assistance Foundation
P.O. Box 877
Concord, NH 03302
603-225-6612

New Jersey
New Jersey Higher Education Assistance Authority
CN 543
Trenton, NJ 08625
609-588-3200

New Mexico
New Mexico Educational Assistance Foundation
P.O. Box 27020
Albuquerque, NM 87125
505-345-3371

New York
New York State Higher Education Services Corporation
99 Washington Ave.
Albany, NY 12255
518-473-1575

North Carolina
North Carolina State Education Assistance Authority
P.O. Box 2688
Chapel Hill, NC 27515-2688
919-549-8614

North Dakota
Bank of North Dakota
Student Loan Department
Box 5509
Bismarck, ND 58502
701-224-5656

Ohio
Ohio Student Loan Commission
P.O. Box 16610
Columbus, OH 43266-0610
614-644-6627

Oklahoma
Oklahoma State Regents for Higher Education
500 Education Building
State Capitol Complex
Oklahoma City, OK 73105
405-521-8262

Oregon
Oregon State Scholarship Commission
1445 Willamette St.

Suite 9
Eugene, OR 97401
800-452-8807
503-346-3200

Pennsylvania
Pennsylvania Higher Education Assistance Agency
660 Boas St.
Harrisburg, PA 17102
800-692-7392
717-257-2860

Rhode Island
Rhode Island Higher Education Assistance Authority
560 Jefferson Blvd.
Warwick, RI 02886
401-277-2050

South Carolina
South Carolina Student Loan Corporation
Interstate Center
Suite 210
P.O. Box 21487
Columbia, SC 29221
803-798-6423

South Dakota
Education Assistance Corporation
115 First Ave., S.W.
Aberdeen, SD 57401
605-225-6423

Tennessee
Tennessee Student Assistance Corporation
404 James Robertson Parkway
Nashville, TN 37243-0820
615-741-1346

Texas
Texas Guaranteed Student Loan Corporation
P.O. Box 15996
Austin, TX 78761
512-835-1900

Utah
Utah Higher Education Assistance Authority
P.O. Box 45202
Salt Lake City, UT 84145-0202
801-538-5240

Vermont
Vermont Student Assistance Corporation
Champlain Mill
P.O. Box 2000
Winooski, VT 05404
800-642-3177
802-655-9602

Virgina
State Education Assistance Authority
6 N. 6th St.
Suite 300
Richmond, VA 23219
804-786-2035

Washington
Washington Student Loan Guarantee Association
500 Colman Bldg.
811 First Ave.
Seattle, WA 98104
206-625-1030

West Virginia
Higher Education Assistance Foundation
P.O. Box 591
Charleston, WV 25322
304-345-7211

Wisconsin
Wisconsin Higher Education Corporation
2401 International Lane
Madison, WI 53704
608-246-1800

Wyoming
Higher Education Assistance Foundation
American National Bank Building
1912 Capitol Ave.
Suite 320
Cheyenne, WY 82001
307-635-3259

Unsubsidized Stafford Loans

Students who fail to qualify for a need-based Stafford Loan still have the option of applying for an unsubsidized Stafford Loan. These operate identically to subsidized Staffords, with a couple of exceptions. One, the borrowing limit is higher for unsubsidized loans as students progress through four years of undergraduate education. And two, while the interest on subsidized loans does not begin to accrue until a student either graduates or leaves school, the interest on unsubsidized loans begins to accrue immediately. Borrowers do have the option to make monthly interest-only payments while they're still attending school.

Saving Money on Stafford Loans.

If your child obtains a Stafford Loan that's issued by a bank, savings and loan, or other private lending institution, you may be able to save some money. Some of these institutions sell their student loans to the Student Loan Marketing Association (Sallie Mae), the consolidation agency that services about a third of all student loans. If you make your first 24 monthly payments on time, Sallie Mae will forgive that portion of your loan origination fee above $250. If you make your next 24 monthly payments on time, the agency will lower your interest rate two points for the balance of the loan. If you allow them to make electronic deductions from your checking or savings accounts, they'll knock off another quarter of a point. Depending on your total debt, the savings can be in the hundreds or even thousands of dollars.

Most college financial aid offices can provide you with the names of lenders who sell their loans to Sallie Mae. You also can get names from the state guaranty agencies previously listed.

Perkins Loans

Perkins Loans carry very low interest rates (5 percent) and are available to eligible students enrolled in undergraduate, graduate, and professional programs. They are based on need and, like SEOGs, are derived from an allotment of federal funds given to, and distributed by, college financial aid offices. Undergraduates can borrow up to $15,000 for all four years of study, and graduate students can borrow up to $30,000, including Perkins Loans received for undergraduate study. Limits are increased by 20 percent for study abroad.

Students do not apply directly for Perkins Loans. Rather, they are distributed according to the discretion of financial aid officers when putting together financial aid packages. The eligibility requirements are the same as those for a Pell Grant. Repayment begins six months after a student leaves school (again, graduation is immaterial), and the minimum monthly payment is $40, or $480 a year. As with Stafford Loans, there are conditions in which a Perkins Loan debt may be forgiven.

Work-Study Programs

Here's a way your child can help pay for college. Federal work-study programs provide undergraduate and graduate students with both on- and off-campus jobs. The jobs are often related to a student's career interests and provide him or her with invaluable real-world training. There are usually limits to how much a student can earn, and this figure can change every year. Most earn between $1,000 and $2,000 a year.

Work-study programs are very popular. Since the number of positions is limited at every school, it's important to apply early. The application process varies from school to school, so if you plan on using this strategy, find out as much as you can when you're still researching various schools.

One consideration parents often have is how having a job will affect their child's academic performance. You'll be relieved to learn that it's rarely a problem. In fact, many students actually perform better when they have a part-time job. They learn to ration their time and make better use of their time. The result is usually better study habits and higher grades. I have a daughter who's a college sophomore and works 15 hours a week at the front desk in the lobby of her dormitory. She has a 3.72 GPA and is a Dean's List student.

Paul Douglas Teacher Scholarship Program

This very generous program provides scholarships to high school seniors who are planning careers as teachers. The awards are based on financial need and can be as much as $5,000 per year for four years of undergraduate work. There is a catch, however. For each year the scholarship is received, the recipient agrees to spend two years teaching somewhere in the United States. The commitment can be cut in half by teaching in an area that has been identified as suffering from a shortage of teachers. If a person fails to honor their teaching commitment, the scholarship is considered a loan and must be paid back.

Applications for Douglas Scholarships can be obtained from high school guidance counselors and college financial aid offices. They can also be obtained by writing the Department of Education, 400 Maryland Ave., N.W., Washington, DC 20202.

National Science Scholars Program

High school seniors who have achieved academic excellence in mathematics, engineering, or the physical, life, or computer sciences are eligible for awards from this program. The scholarships award as much as $5,000 a year for undergraduate study. Information on this program can be obtained from high school guidance counselors and college financial aid officers.

AmeriCorps

This program is designed to let students work for two years to save money for college. They are required to work 1,700 hours a year for two years. Each year they earn $4,725 plus another $7,400 in living allowances. They also receive health and child care benefits. For more information, contact the Federal Student Aid Information Center at 800-433-3243 or the White House Office of National Service, OEOB Room 145, Washington, DC 20500.

Parent Loans to Undergraduate Students (PLUS)

The PLUS program provides financial assistance to families who don't qualify for other types of federal assistance, regardless of income. Families can borrow the total amount needed to pay for college less the value of any financial aid received. Interest rates vary but are capped at 10 percent. The loans are made by banks, credit unions, savings and loans, and the states.

Understandably, PLUS loans frequently involve a credit check, so you may find yourself turned down or limited in the amount you can borrow. There are also origination fees and insurance fees. Still, these loans are a good source of funds should you find yourself coming up short of what you need.

Repayment of PLUS loans begins 60 days after the loan is made, and the minimum annual repayment is $600. You can take up to 10 years to repay the loans. There also are conditions under which the loans can be forgiven.

Direct Student Loan Program (DSLP)

DSLP loans are made up of Federal Direct Stafford Loans (subsidized and unsubsidized) and Federal Direct PLUS Loans. They are obtained directly from colleges and universities.

The Reserve Officers Training Corps (ROTC)

After hitting a few low points in the '70s and early '80s, ROTC is back and as popular as ever. Simply put, ROTC is a deal with the armed services. They'll cover anywhere from 80 to 100 percent of your child's college costs in return for your child's service as a commissioned officer after graduation. The government awards more than $125 million in ROTC scholarships every year.

The qualifications for ROTC are tough. Applicants must be in excellent physical condition and equally impressive academic condition—the minimum combined SAT is 1,250. The government prefers applicants who have an interest in math, engineering, science, or technology. Athletes are also popular. The various branches of the armed forces can provide you with a list of schools that sponsor ROTC programs. High school guidance offices also have information.

After graduation, the terms of service are different for each branch of the armed services. Air Force ROTC graduates are required to serve four years of active duty. The navy requires anywhere from four to eight years, depending on the graduate's assignment. The army requires an eight-year commitment. However, they can be eight years of active duty, eight years of reserve duty, or four years of each.

The Service Academies

The U.S. Military Academy at West Point, New York; the U.S. Naval Academy at Annapolis, Maryland; and the U.S. Air Force Academy at Colorado Springs, Colorado, are as difficult to enter as any of the Ivies. But once your child is in, it's a free ride all the way. Tuition, books, fees, and room and board are all covered. Cadets also get a modest salary, not to mention a top-notch education

The catch, as you might have guessed, is a commitment to serve a certain period of time as a commissioned officer once one graduates. The navy and air force require six years of active duty, and the army requires six years of active duty and two years of reserve duty. It's a long commitment, but for the right students, it's a wonderful opportunity.

To be considered for admission, candidates must be nominated by their U.S. Senator or Representative or other individual with nomination rights. Only the very top students are considered, and they all must pass a physical fitness test and meet certain height and weight requirements. The final selection process is rigorous, with about 15 percent of those nominated being admitted.

There are two other service academies, the U.S. Coast Guard Academy at New London, Connecticut, and the U.S. Merchant Marine Academy at Kings Point, New York. The Coast Guard Academy has a conventional college application process and doesn't involve political nomination. The Merchant Marine Academy, however, has the same nomination process as the Big Three academies. The two academies have an annual fee, still less than $1,000, but all other costs are covered.

For information on admission to the service academies, contact the following:

Director of Admissions
U.S. Air Force Academy
Colorado Springs, CO 80840-5651
303-472-2520

Director of Admissions
U.S. Military Academy
600 Thayer Rd.
West Point, NY 10996-1797
914-938-4041

Candidate Guidance Office
U.S. Naval Academy
Leahy Hall
Annapolis, MD 21402-5000
410-293-4361

Director of Admissions
U.S. Coast Guard Academy
New London, CT 06320
203-444-8501

Director of Admissions
U.S. Merchant Marine Academy
Kings Point, NY 11024-1699
516-773-5391

For More Information

The Student Guide: Federal Financial Aid Programs provides more information on federal financial assistance, including eligibility. Write to the Federal Student Aid Information Center, P.O. Box 84, Washington, DC 20044. Phone 800-433-3243.

STATE FINANCIAL AID PROGRAMS

The states also offer a wide range of financial aid programs for college-bound students. All states offer need-based assistance, and many provide grants and scholarships. Depending on what state you live in, you may also find one or more of the following programs.

Work-study programs operate like federal work-study programs and provide part-time employment opportunities for students during the school year.

Prepaid tuition plans allow you to put money aside with the state for your child's future tuition and guarantee the current tuition rate. (We'll look at those closely in chapter 16. They're not all they're cracked up to be.)

Guaranteed tuition plans guarantee that the state will pay the college costs for moderate- and low-income students who qualify for college.

Special loan programs offer low-cost loans for students attending private colleges and universities within the state.

Loan forgiveness programs allow graduates who go into certain professions, such as teaching and health care, to walk away from their state-backed loans.

Tuition equalization programs allow participants to reduce the cost differences between state and private colleges.

Each state maintains special scholarship and grant programs directed at students from different backgrounds or enrolled in different fields of study. Listing them all in this book is impossible, so I've included the names, addresses, and phone numbers of each state's scholarship and loan agencies. Contact them for a complete listing and application information. I've also included the approximate annual amount of student aid each state has made available in recent years.

Alabama
•Scholarships, Grants, and Loans
Alabama Commission on Higher Education
1 Court Square, Suite 221
Montgomery, AL 36197-0001
205-269-2700

Need-based aid: $4,500,000
Merit-based aid: $6,630,000
Other: $4,750,000

Alaska
•Scholarships, Grants, and Loans
Alaska Commission on Post Secondary Education
400 Willoughby Ave.
Box FP
Juneau, AK 99811
901-465-2854

Need-based aid: $475,000
Merit-based aid: $2,000,000

Arizona
•Scholarships and Grants
Arizona Commission for Post Secondary Education
3030 North Central Ave., Suite 1407
Phoenix, AZ 85012
602-255-3109

•Loans
Arizona Educational Loan Program
1400 E. Southern Ave., Suite 200
Tempe, AZ 85282
800-352-3033
602-831-9988

Need-based aid: $3,425,000
Merit-based aid: none

Arkansas
•Scholarships and Grants
Arkansas Department of Higher Education
1220 W. Third St.
Little Rock, AR 72201
506-324-9300

•Loans
Student Loan Guarantee Foundation of Arkansas
219 S. Victory
Little Rock, AR 72201
501-372-1491

Need-based aid: $4,200,000
Merit-based aid: $[illegible]00,000

California
•Scholarships and Grants
California Student Aid Commission
P.O. Box 51084
Sacramento, CA 94245
916-445-0880

•Loans
California Student Aid Commission
1515 S Street
Sacramento, CA 94245
916-323-0435

Need-based aid: $165,000,000
Merit-based aid: none

Colorado
•Scholarships and Grants
Colorado Commission on Higher Education
1300 Broadway, 2nd Floor
Denver, CO 80203
303-866-2723

•Loans
Colorado Guaranteed Student Loan Program
11990 Grant, Suite 500
North Glenn, CO 80233
303-450-9333

Need-based aid: $12,000,000
Merit-based: $11,000,000
Other: $1,250,000

Connecticut
•Scholarships and Grants
Connecticut Department of Higher Education
61 Woodland Station
Hartford, CT 06105
203-566-2618

•Loans
Connecticut Student Loan Foundation
25 Pratt St.
Hartford, CT 06103
203-547-1510

Need-based aid: $21,000,000
Merit-based aid: $200,000
Other: $15,150,000

Delaware
•Scholarships, Grants, and Loans
Delaware Post Secondary Education Committee
Carvel State Office Building
820 N. French St., 4th Floor
Wilmington, DE 19801
Loan information-302-571-6055
Grant information-302-571-3240

Need-based aid: $1,500,000
Merit-based aid: $200,000
Other: $200,000

District of Columbia
•Scholarships and Grants
Office of Post Secondary Education, Research, and Assistance
Department of Human Services
1331 H Street, N.W.
Suite 600
Washington, DC 20005
202-727-3688

•Loans
Higher Education Loan Program
1023 15th St., N.W.
Tenth Floor, Suite 1000
Washington, DC 20005
202-289-4500

Need-based aid: $975,000
Merit-based aid: none

Florida
•Scholarships, Grants, and Loans
Office of Student Financial Assistance
Department of Education
Florida Education Center
Suite 1334
Tallahassee, FL 32399
Loan information-904-488-8093
Grant information-904-488-6181

Need-based aid: $27,000,000
Merit-based aid: $42,000,000

Georgia
•Scholarships, Grants, and Loans
Board of Regents
University System of Georgia
244 Washington St., S.W.
Atlanta, GA 30334
Loan information-404-493-5468
Grant information-404-493-5444

Need-based aid: $5,200,000
Merit-based aid: $16,300,000
Other: $1,575,000

Hawaii
•Scholarships and Grants
State Post Secondary Education Commission
209 Bachman Hall
University of Hawaii
2444 Dole St.
Honolulu, HI 96822
808-948-8213

•Loans
Hawaii Education Loan Program
P.O. Box 22187
Honolulu, HI 96822
808-536-3731

Need-based aid: $615,000
Merit-based aid: none

Idaho
•Scholarships and Grants
Office of the State Board of Education of Idaho
650 W. State St., Room 307
Boise, ID 83720
208-334-2270

•Loans
Student Loan Fund Processing Center
P.O. Box 730
Fruitland, ID 83619
208-452-4058

Need-based aid: $500,000
Merit-based aid: $250,000

Illinois
•Scholarships, Grants, and Loans
Illinois State Scholarship Commission
106 Wilmot Rd.
Deerfield, IL 60015
708-948-8550

Need-based aid: $180,500,000
Merit-based aid: $18,300,000

Indiana
•Scholarships, Grants, and Loans
State Student Assistance Commission of Indiana
964 N. Pennsylvania St.
Indianapolis, IN 46204
Loan information-317-232-2366
Grant information-317-232-2350

Need-based aid: $46,500,000
Merit-based aid: $975,000

Iowa
•Scholarships, Grants, and Loans
Iowa College Aid Commission
201 Jewett Building
9th and Grand
Des Moines, IA 50309
Loan information-515-281-4890
Grant information-515-281-3501

Need-based aid: $37,750,000
Merit-based aid: $900,000

Kansas
•Scholarships and Grants
Kansas Board of Regents
Capitol Tower, Suite 609
400 S.W. 8th
Topeka, KS 66603
913-296-3517

•Loans
Higher Education Assistance Foundation
6800 College Blvd., Suite 600
Overland Park, KS 66211
913-345-1300

Need-based aid: $6,600,000
Merit-based aid: $30,000
Other: $50,000

Kentucky
•Scholarships, Grants, Loans
Kentuckey Higher Education Assistance Authority
1050 U.S. 127 South, Suite 102
West Frankfort, KY 40601
502-564-7990

Need-based aid: $19,400,000
Merit-based aid: none

Louisiana
•Scholarships, Grants, and Loans
Louisiana Student Financial Assistance Special Commission
P.O. Box 91202
Baton Rouge, LA 70821-9202
504-342-9415

Need-based aid: $4,200,000
Merit-based aid: $775,000

Maine
•Scholarships, Grants, and Loans
Maine Dept. of Educational and Cultural Services
Division of Higher Education Services
State House Station 119
Augusta, ME 04333
800-228-3734
207-289-2183

Need-based aid: $5,100,000
Merit-based aid: none

Maryland
•Scholarships and Grants
Maryland Higher Education Commission
16 Francis St.
Annapolis, MD 21401-1781
410-974-5370

•Loans
Maryland Higher Education Loan Corporation
2100 Guilford Ave., Room 305
Baltimore, MD 21218
410-333-6555

Need-based aid: $15,750,000
Merit-based aid: $5,150,000

Massachusetts
•Scholarships and Grants
The Board of Regents of Higher Education
Scholarship Office
150 Causeway St., Room 600
Boston, MA 02114
617-727-9420

•Loans
Massachusetts Higher Education Assistance Corporation
Berkeley Place
330 Stuart St.
Boston, MA 02116
617-426-9796

Need-based aid: $53,300,000
Merit-based aid: $50,000
Other: $18,650,000

Michigan
•Scholarships and Grants
Michigan Department of Education
P.O. Box 3008
Lansing, MI 48909
517-373-3394

•Loans
Michigan Department of Education
Guaranteed Student Loan Program
Box 30047
Lansing, MI 48909
517-373-0760

Need-based aid: $73,200,000
Merit-based aid: none
Other: $1,700,000

Minnesota
•Scholarships and Grants
Minnesota Higher Education Coordinating Board
Capitol Square, Suite 400
550 Cedar St.
St. Paul, MN 55101
612-296-3974

•Loans
Higher Education Assistance Foundation
85 E. Seventh St., Suite 500

St. Paul, MN 55101
612-227-7661

Need-based aid: $76,000,000
Merit-based aid: none
Other: $1,750,000

Mississippi
•Scholarships and Grants
Board of Trustees of State Institutions of Higher Learning
P.O. Box 2336
Jackson, MS 39225-2336
601-982-6570

•Loans
Mississippi Guarantee Student Loan Agency
3825 Ridgewood Rd.
P.O. Box 342
Jackson, MS 39211-6453
601-982-6570

Need-based aid: $11,350,000
Merit-based aid: $700,000

Missouri
•Scholarships, Grants, and Loans
Coordinating Board for Higher Education
P.O. Box 1438
Jefferson City, MO 65102
314-751-3940

Need-based aid: $1[illegible],150,000
Merit-based aid: $10,100,000
Other $260,000

Montana
•Scholarships, Grants, and Loans
Montana Guaranteed Student Loan Program
33 S. Last Chance Gulch
Helena, MT 59620
406-444-6594

Need-based aid: $385,000
Merit-based aid: none

Nebraska
•Scholarships and Grants
Nebraska Coordinating Commission for Post Secondary Education
Sixth Floor State Capitol
P.O. Box 95005
Lincoln, NE 68509
402-471-2847

•Loans
Higher Education Assistance Foundation
Cornhusker Bank Building
Suite 304
11th & Cornhusker Hwy.
Lincoln, NE 68521
402-476-9129

Need-based aid: $2,200,000
Merit-based aid: none

Nevada
•Scholarships and Grants
Student Services
Office of Student Financial Services
University of Nevada at Reno
Room 200 TSSC
Reno, NV 89557
702-784-4666

•Loans
Nevada State Department of Education
400 W. King St.
Capitol Complex
Carson City, NV 89710
702-885-5914

Need-based aid: $400,000
Merit-based aid: none

New Hampshire
•Scholarships and Grants
New Hampshire Post Secondary Education Commission
Two Industrial Park Drive
Concord, NH 03301-9681
603-271-2555

•Loans
New Hampshire Higher Education Assistance Foundation
P.O. Box 877
Concord, NH 03302
800-235-2577

Need-based aid: $775,000
Merit-based aid: $10,000
Other: $700,000

New Jersey
•Scholarships and Grants
Department of Higher Education
Office of Student Assistance
CN 540
Trenton, NJ 08625
800-962-4636

•Loans
New Jersey Higher Education Assistance Authority
CN 543
Trenton, NJ 08625
609-588-3200

Need-based aid: $96,000,000
Merit-based aid: $6,250,000

New Mexico
Scholarships and Grants
Commission on Higher Education
1068 Cerillos Rd.
Santa Fe, NM 87501
505-827-8300

•Loans
New Mexico Educational Assistance Foundation
P.O. Box 27020
Albuquerque, NM 87125
505-345-3371

Need-based aid: $7,250,000
Merit-based aid: $4,000,000
Other: $2,175,000

New York
•Scholarships, Grants, and Loans
New York State Higher Education Services Corporation
99 Washington Ave.
Albany, NY 12255
Loan information-518-473-1574
Grant information-518-474-5642

Need-based aid: $406,000,000
Merit-based aid: $30,000,000

North Carolina
•Scholarships, Grants, and Loans
North Carolina State Education Assistance Authority
P.O. Box 2688
Chapel Hill, NC 27515-2688
919-549-8614

Need-based aid: $3,700,000
Merit-based aid: $24,500,000
Other: $30,000,000

North Dakota
•Scholarships and Grants
North Dakota Student Financial Assistance Program
State Capitol, 10th Floor
Bismarck, ND 58505-0154
701-224-4114

•Loans
Bank of North Dakota
Student Loan Department
Box 5509
Bismarck, ND 58502
701-224-5600

Need-based aid: $1,200,000
Merit-based aid: $290,000

Ohio
•Scholarships and Grants
Ohio Board of Regents
Student Assistance Office
3600 State Office Tower
30 E. Broad St.
Columbus, OH 43266-0417
614-466-7420

•Loans
Ohio Student Loan Commission
P.O. Box 16610
Columbus, OH 43266-0610
614-644-6627

Need-based aid: $52,775,000
Merit-based aid: $27,250,000

Oklahoma
•Scholarships, Grants, and Loans
Oklahoma State Regents for Higher Education
500 Education Building
State Capitol Complex
Oklahoma City, OK 73105
Loan information-405-521-8262
Grant information-405-525-8180

Need-based aid: $13,250,000
Merit-based aid: $3,200,000
Other: $18,750,000

Oregon
•Scholarships, Grants, and Loans
Oregon State Scholarship Commission
1445 Willamette St.
Suite 9
Eugene, OR 97401
800-452-8807
Loan information-503-686-3200
Grant information-503-686-4166

Pennsylvania
•Scholarships, Grants, and Loans
Pennsylvania Higher Education Assistance Agency
660 Boas St.
Harrisburg, PA 17102
Loan information-800-692-7392
Grant information-800-692-7435

Need-based aid: $145,000,000
Merit-based aid: $635,000

Rhode Island
•Scholarships, Grants, and Loans
Rhode Island Higher Education Assistance Authority
560 Jefferson Blvd.
Warwick, RI 02886
401-277-2050
800-922-9855

Need-based aid: $10,000,000
Merit-based aid: $120,000
Other: $425,000

South Carolina
•Scholarships and Grants
Higher Education Tuition Grants Agency
Box 12159
Columbia, SC 29211
803-734-1200

•Loans
South Carolina Student Loan Corporation
Interstate Center
Suite 210
P.O. Box 21487
Columbia, SC 29221
803-798-0916

Need-based aid: $18,000,000
Merit-based aid: none

South Dakota
•Scholarships and Grants
Department of Education and Cultural Affairs
Richard F. Kneip Bldg.
700 Governors Dr.
Pierre, SD 57501-2293
650-773-3134

•Loans
Education Assistance Corporation
115 First Ave., S.W.
Aberdeen, SD 57401
605-225-6423

Need-based aid: $460,000
Merit-based aid: $90,000

Tennessee
•Scholarships, Grants, and Loans
Tennessee Student Assistance Corporation
404 James Robertson Parkway
Nashville, TN 37243-0820
800-342-1663
615-741-1346

Need-based aid: $14,200,000
Merit-based aid: $570,000
Other: $3,275,000

Texas
•Scholarships and Grants
Texas Higher Education Coordinating Board
P.O. Box 12788
Austin, TX 78711
512-462-6400

•Loans
Texas Guaranteed Student Loan Corporation
P.O. Box 15996
Austin, TX 78761
512-835-1900

Need-based aid: $27,300,000
Merit-based aid: none
Other: $91,000,000

Utah
•Scholarships and Grants
Utah State Board of Regents
3 Triad Center, Suite 550
335 W. North Temple
Salt Lake City, UT 84180-1205
801-538-5247

•Loans
Loan Servicing Corporation of Utah
P.O. Box 30802
Salt Lake City, UT 84130-0802
801-363-9151

Need-based aid: $1,000,000
Merit-based aid: $985,000
Other: $9,500,000

Vermont
•Scholarships, Grants, and Loans
Vermont Student Assistance Corporation
Champlain Mill
P.O. Box 2000
Winooski, VT 05404
800-642-3177
802-655-9602

Need-based aid: $11,000,000
Merit-based aid: none
Other: $200,000

Virginia
•Scholarships and Grants
Virginia Education Loan Authority
One Franklin Square
411 E. Franklin St.
Richmond, VA 23219
800-792-5626

•Loans
State Education Assistance Authority
6 N. 6th St.
Suite 300
Richmond, VA 23219
804-786-2035

Need-based aid: $7,500,000
Merit-based aid: $18,100,000

Washington
•Scholarships and Grants
Washington Higher Education Coordinating Board
917 Lakeridge Way
Olympia, WA 98504
206-753-3571

•Loans
Washington Student Loan Guarantee Association
500 Colman Bldg.
811 First Ave.
Seattle, WA 98104
206-625-1030

Need-based aid: $21,125,000
Merit-based aid: $32,000
Other: $875,000

West Virginia
•Scholarships and Grants
West Virginia Higher Education Central Office
P.O. Box 4007
Charleston, WV 25364
304-347-1231

•Loans
Higher Education Assistance Foundation
P.O. Box 591
Charleston, WV 25322
304-345-7211

Need-based aid: $5,500,000
Merit-based aid: none
Other: $7,400,000

Wisconsin
•Scholarships and Grants
Wisconsin Higher Education Aids Board
P.O. Box 7885
Madison, WI 53707-7885
608-267-2206

•Loans
Wisconsin Higher Education Corporation
2401 International Lane
Madison, WI 53704
608-246-1800

Need-based aid: $42,000,000
Merit-based aid: $700,000
Other: $2,000,000

Wyoming
•Scholarships and Grants
Wyoming Community College Commission
122 W. 25th St.
Herschler Bldg.
Cheyenne, WY 82002
307-777-7763

•Loans
Higher Education Assistance Foundation
American National Bank Building
1912 Capitol Ave.
Suite 320
Cheyenne, WY 82001
307-635-3259

Need-based aid: $240,000
Merit-based aid: none

COLLEGE AND UNIVERSITY FINANCIAL AID PROGRAMS

The federal and state governments may be the two biggest sources of financial aid for college students, but colleges and universities do what they can, too. In fact, they're quite generous. More than 85 percent offer some form of financial aid to their students.

As you might expect, the amount of assistance they can offer is all over the board. A good indicator of how much financial aid a school can afford is its endowment per student. Most financial aid is generated by endowment, so the higher the endowment per student, the greater the amount of money that's generated per student. For example, in 1995–96, Princeton University had an endowment of $701,000 per student, the highest in the nation. If the endowment was earning 10 percent (which it better have, considering the way the market performed during that time), that means that Princeton's administrators had an astonishing $70,000 to spend for each of its students. And that's just earnings from endowment. It doesn't include tuition, fees, federal and state funding, and other sources of income.

At the other end of the spectrum are junior colleges and other small schools that don't even have endowments. Any financial aid they can offer might be solely through federal and state contributions.

Obtaining Financial Aid from a School

As I pointed out earlier, the first step in getting financial aid of any type is to file a federal FAFSA application. Colleges and universities want to know that you've exhausted your federal and state options before they'll part with any money.

Ask about financial aid policies when you're first looking at schools. What kinds of assistance do they offer? Do they completely cover the financial needs of their students or just part of it? What percentage of aid is given in grants? In scholarships? In loans? Do they offer aid all four years? What's the average indebtedness of the school's students when they graduate?

Here are some of the ways you can obtain financial aid from colleges and universities.

Grants.

Like federal and state grants, most college grants are need-based. The financial aid office at each school can provide you with specific requirements for eligibility.

Scholarships.

Look at scholarships particularly carefully. While most grants are based on financial need, scholarships are awarded for academic achievement, athletic prowess, and other talents. They can save you a lot of money.

For example, my daughter was a National Merit Scholar in high school and scored 1370 on her SATs. She's now attending a state university in the Midwest. Because of her high SAT scores, she qualified for in-state tuition, even though we live in New York. She also receives $750 a year from her National Merit Scholarship. But she didn't get the best news until she arrived on campus her first year. Her advisor informed her that because she's a National Merit Scholar, she qualifies for a $5,000-a-year scholarship from the State Board of Regents. So between the in-state tuition, the National Merit Scholarship, and the Regents Scholarship, she has just about all the bases covered. Her freshman year only cost us about $2,500, and most of that was for travel expenses and incidentals.

So high school performance, high school rank, ACT scores, SAT scores, and other academic measures can all help your child land a scholarship. So can athletic ability. Division I colleges and universities dole out thousands of "full ride" scholarships every year to athletes in major sports like football and basketball. The practice pays for itself because of the enormous income these sports generate for the school. But athletes in less popular sports like swimming, track and field, lacrosse, ice hockey, and wrestling can also earn scholarships at schools with competitive programs.

Although academic and athletic talents land the majority of scholarships, other abilities can be rewarded as well. There are scholarships for music, art, drama, and other disciplines. There are also scholarships for women and various ethnic groups (we'll look at these in the next chapter).

When you're researching colleges and universities, look for schools that offer scholarships that meet your child's talents. Find out how much of the total cost they cover, if they are renewable, and what you have to do to renew them.

Loans.

Quite a number of schools have developed loan programs for families that don't meet federal or state loan requirements. Amherst College, for example, offers loans of up to $10,400 each year to students and their families. The only problem is that the interest rate on the loans offered by schools is usually higher than that for federal and state loans. These loans should only be considered as a fallback strategy when other sources of financial aid fall through.

Employee tuition assistance programs.

If you're an employee of a college or university, whether faculty or staff, you more than likely get a discount on tuition if your child attends your school. A number of schools also contribute to the tuition of their employees' children even when they enroll at other colleges.

Discount programs.

If you have more than one child of college age, you may be able to save money if they attend the same school. Many schools will give a tuition discount to second and third children. Some also give discounts to the children of alumni.

OTHER SOURCES OF FINANCIAL AID

The financial aid sources we've looked at so far in this chapter—the federal and state governments and colleges and universities themselves—make up the bulk of the financial aid system in the United States. But there are more than 300,000 individual scholarship and grant programs sponsored by organizations like Rotary International and the Elks, as well as corporations like Coca-Cola and General Motors. Finding the ones that match your child's needs and talents takes time and a bit of research but, believe me, it's worth it.

To get an idea of just how much money you can garner with a little effort, consider Marianne Ragins of Macon, Georgia. She's one of five children of a widowed mother and had enormous financial needs. So she started researching financial aid sources. By the time she stopped writing letters and making phone calls and filling out applications, she had racked up more than $400,000 in scholarships, $125,000 of which she used to attend Florida A&M University. She's written a book, *Winning Scholarships for College: An Insider's Edge* (Owlet, 1994), that lists 100 scholarship sources and tips on how to apply for them. (I've also listed a number of excellent reference sources for scholarships at the end of this chapter.)

National Merit Scholarships.

Every year, 15,000 high school students who perform well on the PSATs are selected as semifinalists for National Merit Scholarships. These awards total about $21 million and are funded by approximately 200 schools and 400 companies. Ultimately, about 6,500 students will be awarded scholarships ranging from $250 to $2,500. In addition to their test scores, they're evaluated on community service, academic performance, and recommendations from teachers.

The Coca-Cola Scholars Foundation.

Every year, this organization awards grants of $20,000 each to 50 high school seniors. Qualifications for the grants include academic achievement, leadership, and civic responsibility. In addition, another 100 semifinalists receive $4,000 each.

The Westinghouse Science Talent Search.

Westinghouse invites approximately 1,500 participants in high school science fairs to submit research projects in science, math, or technology for this competition. Ten winners receive awards of from $10,000 to $40,000. Another 30 runners-up receive $1,000 apiece.

The Tylenol Scholarship Fund.

Sponsored by McNeil Consumer Products, the company that manufactures Tylenol, this fund annually awards $10,000 scholarships to 10 high school seniors who demonstrate academic achievement, leadership skills, and contribute to their communities. Five hundred semifinalists receive $1,000 each.

These programs are among the most generous—and selective—in the country. Most scholarships are for less money. But with some effort you and your child can put together your own financial aid "package" that will put a significant dent in your college costs. If you're lucky, you might be able to cover everything.

The lesson to be learned here is to conduct your own research. Start early, and turn over every stone you can find. There's a wealth of financial aid money out there. There's so much, in fact, that more than 3 percent goes unclaimed every year. That's several million dollars, enough to cover the costs of several hundred students. Some of it could be yours.

OTHER SOURCES OF LOANS

If you don't qualify for a low-interest government loan but still need to come up with some cash, there are a number of private loan programs that can help you. Most will lend you most or all of the money you need at relatively reasonable interest rates and with long repayment schedules.

Obviously, a good credit history is a must in obtaining these loans, so you might want to check your credit history before you start filling out applications. Contact the three major credit reporting agencies: TRW (800-392-1122), TransUnion (216-779-7200), and Equifax (800-685-1111). TRW will give you one report a year for free. The other two agencies charge a fee.

These loans aren't the perfect solution to the problem, but they're better than nothing. Here are a few of the most popular.

The Education Resources Institute (TERI)

TERI is the nation's largest private educational lender. You can borrow up to the total cost of your child's education and have up to 25 years for repayment. The terms vary and are dictated by the program's sponsors, most of whom are banks. You can get a list of lenders in your area by calling 800-255-8374.

The New England Loan Marketing Association (Nellie Mae)

This organization offers loans of from $2,000 to the full cost of your child's education, less financial aid. Interest rates are usually 2 to 4 percent above the prime rate plus an initial fee of 5 percent of the amount of the loan. Repayment can be as long as 20 years. For information, call Nellie Mae at 800-634-9308.

The College Board

This organization offers a couple of plans. The first, the Extra Credit Loan, covers all costs less financial aid for up to 4 years and gives you up to 15 years for repayment. The second, the Extra Time Loan, allows you to borrow a year at a time. Repayment can be made over 10 years, and you can wait until your child graduates to begin repayment of the principal. Interest rates are tied to the 90-day Treasury bill plus 4.5 percent. Call 800-874-9390 for more information.

The College Resource Center

This organization will loan you a maximum of $50,000. There is an application fee of 3 percent of the value of the loan, and interest rates can be as low as the prime rate plus 2.5 percent. Repayment begins within 45 days, and the minimum monthly amount is $100 a month or 2 percent of the outstanding balance, whichever is greater. For information, call 800-477-4977.

ONE STUDENT'S FINANCIAL AID STORY

When Andrea Garcia of Harlingen, Texas, was looking at colleges a few years ago, she quickly narrowed down her choices to two—Baylor University in Waco, a few hours from her home, and Cornell University in Ithaca, New York, more than 1,700 miles from her home. When it came time to make her decision, however, it was financial aid, not location, that made the difference.

She chose Cornell, the Ivy League school known for bending over backward to make sure deserving students get the money they need to come there. The university put together a financial aid package that included Federal Pell Grants, Federal Perkins and Stafford Loans, Cornell grants, and a work-study program that completely covered her tuition, fees, and room and board. Her contribution and that of her parents covers books, travel expenses, and incidental expenses. Baylor's offer paled in comparison, covering only half her tuition.

The child of a hospital safety officer and a paraprofessional, Andrea is an entomology major with a minor in photography. She says it would have been impossible to attend a major university like Cornell without financial aid. Her parents' combined annual income is about $40,000, and she has two younger brothers, one of whom is also in college.

Andrea's Pell Grant and Cornell grants cover slightly more than $13,000 of her approximately $22,000 annual college costs. The rest is covered by her Stafford and Perkins Loans. The work-study portion of her package employs her 14 hours a week in the photography unit of Cornell's Office of University Relations. She helps with paperwork, files photos, and takes care of whatever other tasks need doing. The money she earns helps pay bills and other personal expenses not covered by her grants and loans.

Despite the financial aid she's received, Andrea will be more than $40,000 in debt when she graduates. Is it worth it?

"It is worth it, but it does scare me," she admits. "If I was going to be a doctor or a lawyer it might not bother me so much. But I'm a bug person, and I don't see myself making a lot of money, at least not very soon."

Did Andrea make any mistakes in the financial aid process? Yes. She relied totally on Cornell's Financial Aid Office to put together her financial aid package and didn't do any research on her own. If she had, she might have discovered other grant or scholarship opportunities that would have reduced the amount of federal loan assistance she needed. That, in turn, would have reduced her debt when she graduates.

But she's also doing something right. As I mentioned earlier in the chapter, there are certain conditions under which Perkins and Stafford Loans can be forgiven. When I last talked to her, Andrea was getting ready to visit her financial aid officer to see what exactly she has to do to get her debts canceled.

RIGHTS AND RESPONSIBILITIES

The offer and acceptance of financial aid, whether a grant, scholarship, or loan, carries with it certain rights and responsibilities on the part of both the student and the college or university.

All schools have their own financial aid philosophies and practices. These are written statements and are available from financial aid offices. Both you and your child have the responsibility to understand what they are when you begin the financial aid application process. You need to find out what kinds of financial aid the schools offer, how they determine what constitutes an individual's financial aid package, whether they sponsor their own loan programs, and other information. You also need to find out what their refund policies are.

Many times a student's financial aid package will be worth less than he or she had hoped. All schools have an appeals process through which any student who wishes to contest their award can do so. Most schools require little more than a signed letter explaining the student's financial situation and why they feel they should be granted a larger award. After the letter is received, a personal meeting between the student and a financial aid officer is sometimes held.

The appeals process is important and should not be ignored out of concern that your child will be labeled a troublemaker. Financial aid officers go out of their way to help students meet their proven financial needs. Sometimes there's simply just not enough money to go around. If that's the case, the financial aid officer may be able to suggest alternative loan sources or job opportunities.

Students' Rights

- Students have the right to know what financial aid programs are available from their college or university.
- Students have the right to know the deadlines for submitting applications.
- Students have the right to know how their financial need was determined and what items were considered from their budget.
- Students have the right to know how their financial aid will be distributed.

- Students have the right to know their college or university's institutional financial aid philosophy and packaging guidelines.
- Students have the right to know their college's or university's appeals process.
- Students have the right to know their college's or university's refund policy.
- Students have the right to know what portion of their aid package is a loan and must be repaid and what portion is a grant or scholarship and does not have to be repaid.
- Students have the right to know the college's or university's definition of and determination of satisfactory academic progress.

Students' Responsibilities

- Students must submit all financial aid application forms with accurate information and by the deadline.
- Students must be truthful on their application forms.
- Students must agree to provide financial aid offices with any additional documentation, verification, corrections, or other information.
- Students must report any change in their family's financial status.
- Students must report and outside loans or scholarships.
- Students must read and understand all the terms and agreements of their financial aid package.
- Students must repay all educational loans.
- Students must read, understand, and keep copies of all forms they sign.
- Students must perform satisfactorily the work agreed upon in a work-study job.
- Students must notify their lenders(s) if they graduate or withdraw from school.
- Students must notify their lender(s) if they transfer to another school.
- Students must notify their lender(s) of any address changes.
- Students must notify their lender(s) if their enrollment drops to less than half-time status.

- Students must notify their lender(s) of anything that might affect their ability to repay a loan or their eligibility for deferment or cancellation.
- Students must attend an exit interview before they leave school if they've borrowed money from federal, state, or school loan sources.

Make sure you and your child understand and follow these rules governing the financial aid agreement. And be honest in your dealings with financial aid offices and other agencies. The risks of being less than honest aren't worth it.

FOR MORE INFORMATION

Here are some books and World Wide Web sites that will help you find grants, scholarships, low-cost loans, and other financial aid information.

- *The Scholarship Book* by Daniel J. Cassidy, Prentice-Hall, 1996.
- *How to Obtain Maximum College Financial Aid* by Edward Rosenwasser, Student College Aid, 1995.
- *Don't Miss Out: The Ambitious Student's Guide to Financial Aid* by Anna Leider and Robert Leider, Dearborn Trade, 1995.
- *How the Military Will Help You Pay for College: The High School Student's Guide to ROTC, the Academies, and Special Programs* by Don Betterton, Peterson's Guides, 1990.
- *The A's and B's of Academic Scholarships,* Debra L. Wexler, editor, Octameron Associates, Dearborn Trade.
- *The Complete Family Guide to College Financial Aid* by Richard Black, Perigee/Berkley Publishing, 1995.
- *College Costs and Financial Aid Handbook,* The College Board, 1996.
- *Financial Aids for Higher Education* by Oreon Keeslar, Brown & Benchmark.
- The Financial Aid Information Page—http://www.finaid.org
- U.S. Department of Education—http://www.easi.ed.gov
- The College Board Web Site—http://www.collegeboard.org
- Kaplan Student Loan Information Program—http://www.kaploan.com

- fastWEB—http://www.studentservices.com/fastweb
- The Student Loan Marketing Association Home Page—http://www.salliemae.com
- Scholarship Resource Network Express—http://www.rams.com/srn/search.htm
- Signet Bank Student Loan Home Page—http://www.jerome.signet.com/collegemoney

WHAT'S NEXT?

Everyone qualifies for the largest sources of federal, state, and school financial aid. But there are also programs aimed specially at three groups for whom access to higher education has not always been equitable—women, minorities, and people with disabilities. We'll look at some of these programs in chapter 12.

12

FINANCIAL ASSISTANCE FOR WOMEN, MINORITIES, AND THE DISABLED

Over the last several decades, the civil rights movement, the women's movement, and a growing awareness of the needs and rights of the disabled have awakened higher education to its responsibilities to these groups. As a result, there are more sources of financial aid for women, minorities, and people with disabilities today than ever before.

FINANCIAL ASSISTANCE PROGRAMS FOR WOMEN

Women can select from a wide variety of financial aid opportunities. The YWCA, the Girl Scouts of America, sororities, business groups, women's clubs, and other organizations offer a wide variety of grants and scholarships to women. Some are based on academic performance and citizenship. Others are based on area of study. Some are awarded solely on need, and others are awarded on merit. There are even financial aid programs for adult women who have either been in the workforce or at home raising families and are now ready to pursue an undergraduate degree.

This is a particularly advantageous time for young women interested in attending women-only colleges. Enrollment in these institutions has been steadily dropping for the last 20 years, and many have gone coed rather than risk financial ruin. Some of the best known women's colleges, such as Vassar and Sarah Lawrence, have enrolled men for a number of years now. But those that still enroll women only offer generous financial aid packages to entice talented students.

Here are some of the organizations that provide financial aid to women.

American Business Women's Association

This organization provides loan and scholarship assistance for qualified women students. Applicants must be U.S. citizens, enrolled in an accredited college, university, or vocational school, and sponsored by a member of the organization. Awards vary in size according to financial need. For information, contact the American Business Women's Association, National Headquarters, 9100 Ward Parkway, P.O. Box 8728, Kansas City, MO 64114. Phone 816–361–6621.

American Council of Independent Laboratories, Inc.

This organization offers scholarships to women in their junior and senior year of college who are pursuing degrees in biology or chemistry. Contact the Scholarship Chairperson, American Council of Independent Laboratories, Inc., 2001 Pine Dr., Lancaster, PA 17601.

American Society of Women Accountants

This group offers scholarships to junior and senior women who are pursuing a degree in accounting. Contact the American Society of Women Accountants, 134 Cliff Ave., Winthrup, MA 02152.

Business and Professional Women's Foundation Loan Fund for Women in Engineering

This fund has been set up to provide financial assistance to women in their final two years of an accredited engineering program. Applicants must be U.S. citizens and demonstrate financial need. For information, contact the Business and Professional Women's Foundation, 2012 Massachusetts Ave., N.W., Washington, DC 20036.

Citizen's Scholarship Foundation of America, Inc.

This organization evaluates applicants and selects recipients for scholarships awarded by corporations, foundations, associations, and other organizations. There is a $2 charge for a list of available scholarships. Contact the Citizen's Scholarship Foundation of

America, Inc., 1505 Riverview Road, P.O. Box 297, Minneapolis, MN 56082.

Daughters of the American Revolution

The DAR provides financial assistance for qualified women students throughout the country. Most of the scholarships are administered by individual state DAR societies, each of which have their own deadlines, etc. A variety of scholarships in varying amounts are available. For information, contact your local DAR chapter or the Office of Committees, 1776 D Street, N.W., Washington, DC 20006.

Daughters of the Cincinnati

This group provides scholarships based on financial need and is limited to high school seniors who are the daughters of active duty or retired officers in the United States Army, Navy, Air Force, Coast Guard, or Marine Corps. Contact the Daughters of the Cincinnati, 122 E. 58th St., New York, NY 10022. Phone 212–319–6915.

General Electric Scholarship Program

GE provides scholarships for first-year women students who are majoring in engineering. Contact the Society of Women Engineers, 345 E. 47th St., New York, NY 10017.

Sid Guber Memorial Award

These awards are administered through the Foundation of American Women in Radio and Television and provide financial assistance to undergraduate and graduate women in the performing arts. For information, contact the Foundation of American Women in Radio and Television, Inc., 1101 Connecticut Ave., Suite 700, Washington, DC 20036.

Jewish Foundation for Education of Women

Women undergraduates, graduate students, and doctoral students qualify for scholarship assistance and loans from this organization. The awards are made on a nonsectarian basis and are based on financial need. Applicants must live within 50 miles of the metropolitan New York area. Contact the Jewish Foundation for Education of Women, 330 W. 58th St., New York, NY 10019. Phone 212–265–2565.

Kappa Kappa Gamma Scholarship Program

Junior and senior undergraduates and graduate students pursuing rehabilitation degrees can qualify for scholarships from this fraternal organization. They must be students on campuses with a Kappa Kappa Gamma chapter. Contact the Kappa Kappa Gamma Fraternity Headquarters, P.O. Box 2079, Columbus, OH 43216.

Helen Miller Malloch Scholarship

These scholarships are for women pursuing careers in journalism. Applicants must be enrolled in a journalism program or already be in the profession. Contact the National Federation of Press Women, Inc., 1105 Main St., P.O. Box 99, Blue Springs, MO 64013.

Massachusetts Federation of Polish Women

This group provides financial assistance to women intending to pursue a medical career. Applicants must be of Polish ancestry. For information, contact the Massachusetts Federation of Polish Women, 300 Sunnymeade Ave., Chicopee, MA 01013.

National Education Foundation

This organization provides financial assistance through the Zeta Beta sorority. Eligibility requirements vary according to academic program. Contact Zeta Beta Sorority, 1734 New Hampshire Ave., N.W., Washington, DC 20009.

National Home Fashions League, Inc.

Women students in the fields of art, crafts, and design are eligible for financial assistance from this organization. Contact the National Home Fashions League, Inc., 107 World Trade Center, P.O. Box 58045, Dallas, TX 75258.

National Society of Professional Engineers

The NSPE provides scholarships to women pursuing degrees in engineering. Applicants must graduate in the top 25 percent of their high school class. For information, contact the National Society of Professional Engineers, 2029 K St., N.W., Washington, DC 20006.

Polish Women's Alliance Scholarship Program

This organization provides financial assistance to women undergraduates. Contact the Polish Women's Alliance of America, 205 S. Northwest Hwy., Park Ridge, IL 60068.

Olive Lynn Salembier Scholarship

These scholarships are available to women pursuing engineering degrees. Applicants must have been out of the job market for at least two years and be enrolled in an undergraduate or graduate program. Contact the Society of Women Engineers, United Engineering Center, Room 305, 345 E. 47th St., New York, NY 10017.

Soroptimist International of the Americas

High school senior women are eligible for financial assistance from this organization. Awards are based on financial need, merit, and community service. Contact the Scholarship Committee, Soroptimist International of the Americas, 161 Walnut St., Philadelphia, PA 19103.

Veterans Administration Dependents Program

The VA offers a number of financial assistance programs to the spouses and children of deceased or disabled veterans. Recipients receive a monthly stipend based upon their student status. For information, contact the Veterans Administration, 810 Vermont Ave., N.W., Washington, DC 20420. Phone 202-292-4120.

FOR MORE INFORMATION

The following organizations can provide you with additional information on financial aid programs for women.

American Association of University Women
Educational Foundation
2401 Virginia Ave., N.W.
Washington, DC 20037

Business and Professional Women's Foundation
2012 Massachusetts Ave., N.W.
Washington, DC 20036

Jewish Foundation for Education of Women
330 W. 58th St.
New York, NY 10019

National Society of the Daughters of the American Revolution
Office of Committees
1776 D Street, N.W.
Washington, DC 20006

Society of Women Engineers
United Engineering Center
345 E. 47th St., Room 305
New York, NY 10017

FINANCIAL ASSISTANCE PROGRAMS FOR MINORITIES

There is much concern among higher education administrators over the slow growth in the number of minority students in colleges and universities. Increasing minority enrollment is one of the top priorities for almost every school in the country (in fact, calling them desperate wouldn't be much of an overstatement), and the availability of an enormous number of grants and scholarships should make college accessible for any qualified minority student. Not only are the regular federal, state, and school sources available but there are also any number of special financial aid programs designed for minority students.

Two of the best sources for information on financial aid for minorities are high school guidance offices and state departments of higher education. One of the first organizations they'll mention is sure to be the National Achievement Scholarship Program for Outstanding Negro Students. This program is administered by the same organization that runs the National Merit Scholarship Program, and it offers 2,000 merit scholarships every year. It also administers awards sponsored by colleges and corporations.

Here are some other sources of financial aid for minorities.

American Institute of Certified Public Accountants

The AICPA provides scholarships to undergraduate minority accounting majors who are United States citizens. For information, contact the Manager of Minority Recruitment, American Institute of Certified Public Accountants, 1211 Avenue of the Americas, New York, NY 10036.

Association of University Programs in Health Administration

This organization provides internship programs to qualified African American, Native American, Asian American, Mexican American and Puerto Rican students. Recipients must be either second- or third-year undergraduates. Awards are based on academic achievement. For information, contact the Association of University Programs in Health Administration, 1911 N. Fort Myer Drive, Arlington, VA 22209.

Bureau of Indian Affairs Higher Education Grant

The Bureau of Indian Affairs provides financial aid to eligible Native American students through this program. The awards are based on financial need. For information, write the Bureau of Indian Affairs Higher Education Grant Program, Bureau of Indian Affairs, 18th and C Streets, N.W. Washington, DC 20245.

Florida Atlantic University

This public university in Boca Raton offers free tuition to every African American student it admits. In 1996–97 this was worth $1,900 a year. To be admitted, a student must have a 3.0 GPA in high school and SAT scores of at least 1,000. Preference is given to in-state residents. For information, contact the admissions office, Florida Atlantic University, P.O. Box 3091, Boca Raton, FL 33431. Phone: 407-367-3040. E-mail: acc@fau.edu.

General Electric Foundation

GE provides funds for African American, Hispanic, and Native American students enrolled in a two-year community college who plan to transfer to a four-year college or university and pursue a degree in engineering or business administration. The program also considers students at historically black colleges. Candidates must be in their second year of college, have a minimum GPA of 3.0, and be nominated by an official of their school. Financial need is also considered. For information, contact the College Scholarship Service, The College Board, 45 Columbus Ave., New York, NY 10023-6992. Phone 212-713-8000.

General Motors Scholarship Program

GM also has a scholarship program for qualified minority students. The program is coordinated with selected colleges and universities in the United States. For information, contact the General Motors Scholarship Program, General Motors Corporation, 8-163 General Motors Building, Detroit, MI 48202.

Indian Education and Psychology Fellowship Program

Supported by the U.S. Department of Education, this program provides scholarships to Native American and Native Alaskan students who are enrolled in accredited undergraduate or graduate school programs in education, psychology, or related fields. For information, contact the U.S. Department of Education, Indian Education and Psychology Fellowship Program, 400 Maryland Ave., S.W., Washington, DC 20202.

Indian Fellowship Program

This program offers fellowships to Native American students enrolled in undergraduate and graduate programs in business administration, engineering, education, law, medicine, and other fields. The awards are based on financial need. For information, contact the Indian Fellowship Program, Office of Indian Education Programs, 1849 C Street, N.W., MS-Room 3525, Washington, DC 20242.

Indian Health Employees Scholarship Fund, Inc.

This organization provides scholarships to Native American students, with a priority to students enrolled in health care programs. Awards are based on financial need. Contact the Executive Secretary, Indian Health Employees Scholarship Fund, Federal Building, Room 309, Aberdeen, SD 57401.

Indian Health Scholarship

This National Health Service Corps program pays tuition and fees for Native American, Native Alaskan, and Aleut students enrolled in schools of health disciplines not included in the National Health Service Corps Scholarship Program. For each year of support, awardees are expected to serve for a year with the Indian Health Service or some other health organization in need of personnel. For information, contact the Indian Health Service, IHSSP/Twinbrook Plaza, Suite 100, Rockville, MD 20857.

League of United Latin American Citizens

This organization awards up to $1,000 to qualified Hispanic students based on financial need. For information, contact the LULAC National Scholarship Fund, National Education Service Centers, 400 First Street, N.W., Washington, DC 20001.

National Achievement Scholarship Program

This program provides grants to African American high school students who have demonstrated outstanding academic achievement. More than 600 scholarships of varying amounts are awarded each year and are based on the results of the Preliminary Scholastic Aptitude Test/National Merit Scholarship Qualifying Test (PSAT/NMSQT). For information, contact National Achievement Scholarship Program, One Rotary Center, 1560 Sherman Ave., Evanston, IL 60201.

National Action Council for Minorities in Engineering

This organization provides financial assistance for undergraduate minority students pursuing degrees in engineering. The majority of funding is directed through incentive grants that are administered by selected engineering schools. For information, contact the National Action Council for Minorities in Engineering, 3 W. 35th St., New York, NY 10001.

National Hispanic Scholarship Fund

This group awards scholarships to Hispanic students based on financial need, academic merit, and personal qualities. For information, contact the National Hispanic Scholarship Fund, P.O. Box 728, Novato, CA 94948.

National Merit Scholarship Program

This program awards scholarships in varying amounts to qualified African American students. Applicants must be enrolled or accepted at an accredited college or university. For information, contact the National Merit Scholarship Corporation, One Rotary Center, 1560 Sherman Ave., Evanston, IL 60201.

National Society of Professional Engineers

The NSPE provides scholarships to minority students who are enrolled in engineering programs. Applicants must be in the top 25 percent of their high school class. For information, contact the

National Society of Professional Engineers, 11 Dupont Circle, Suite 200, Washington, DC 20036.

Native American Seminary Scholarships

These scholarships are awarded to Native Americans, Aleuts, or Native Alaskans who are U.S. citizens and members of the Presbyterian Church. For information, contact the Church Vocations/Committee on Higher Education, 100 Witherspoon St., Louisville, KY 40202-1396.

Jackie Robinson Foundation

Honoring the first African American to play major league baseball, this organization awards scholarships to minority high school seniors who exhibit leadership qualities and high academic achievement and who will be attending four-year colleges and universities. Contact the Jackie Robinson Foundation, 3 W. 35th St., New York, NY 10001.

United Methodist Church

The UMC awards scholarships to qualified minority undergraduate and graduate students. Applicants must be American citizens or permanent residents; Hispanic, Asian, or Native American; and active members of the Methodist Church. For information, contact the United Methodist Church, Board of Higher Education and Ministry, Box 871, Nashville, TN 37202.

United Negro College Fund

The United Negro College Fund awards around 1,000 scholarships every year to students who attend the more than 40 colleges affiliated with the organization. Scholarships are awarded based on academic merit and financial need and can be renewed for three years. The maximum award is $6,250 a year. For more information, contact: the United Negro College Fund, Inc., Educational Services Department, 500 E. 62nd St., New York, NY 10021.

Roy Wilkins Scholarship Program

This program awards scholarships to minority students based on financial need. Contact the NAACP Youth and College Division, 186 Remsen St., Brooklyn, NY 11201.

FOR MORE INFORMATION

The following organizations and publications can provide you with additional information on financial aid for minority students.

Bureau of Indian Affairs
18th and C Sts., N.W.
Washington, DC 20245

Indian Health Service
Parklawn Building, Room 6-12
5600 Fishers Lane
Rockville, MD 20857

National Hispanic Scholarship Fund
P.O. Box 748
San Francisco, CA 94101

National Medical Association
1012 Tenth St., N.W.
Washington, DC 20001

National Research Council
2101 Constitution Ave., N.W.
Washington, DC 20418

Jackie Robinson Foundation
80-90 Eighth Ave.
New York, NY 10011

United Negro College Fund
500 E. 62nd St.
New York, NY 10021

United States Department of Education
Indian Fellowship Program
400 Maryland Ave., S.W.
Washington, DC 20202

- *The Black Student's Guide to Scholarships: 600+ Private Money Sources for Black and Minority Students,* Barry Barkham, editor, Madison, 1996.
- *Money for College: A Guide to Financial Aid for African-American Students* by Erlene B. Wilson, Plume, 1996.
- *Financial Aid for Minorities: Awards Open to Students With Any Major,* Garrett Park Press, 1994.
- *Financial Aid for Minorities in Health Fields,* Garrett Park Press, 1991.
- *Minority Financial Aid Directory: A Guide to More Than 4,000 Education Scholarships, Loans, Grants, and Fellowships* by Lemuel Berry, Kendall Hunt Publishers, 1995.

FINANCIAL ASSISTANCE PROGRAMS FOR STUDENTS WITH DISABILITIES

Every effort is being made these days to make higher education accessible to people with disabilities. Both the federal government and individual state governments offer financial assistance programs. Many foundations and other organizations also provide assistance.

If you have a child with a disability, take extra care in calculating college costs. Disabled students frequently have expenses over and above those of non-disabled students. These can include transportation, special equipment, interpreters, note takers, and personal attendants. It's important to include these costs when calculating how much you'll need for college. Make sure the financial aid director of the college from which you're requesting financial aid is aware of your child's additional expenses.

Here are some of the organizations that sponsor financial aid programs for people with disabilities.

American Council of the Blind

This organization provides scholarships to blind students enrolled in vocational or technical programs at the undergraduate or graduate level. For information, contact the American Council of the Blind, 1010 Vermont Ave., N.W., Washington, DC 20005.

American Foundation for the Blind

This group provides scholarships to blind women. Awards range from $1,000 to $3,000 per academic year. For information, contact the American Foundation for the Blind, 15 W. 16th St., New York, NY 10011.

Alexander Graham Bell Association for the Deaf

Deaf students can qualify for scholarships worth from $500 to $1,000 from this organization. Contact the Alexander Graham Bell Association for the Deaf, 3417 Volta Place, N.W., Washington, DC 20005.

Gallaudet University

Funded by the federal government, Gallaudet is one of the nation's best-known universities for the deaf. It offers both undergraduate and graduate programs. Contact the Office of Admissions, Gallaudet University, 800 Florida Ave., N.E., Washington, DC 20002.

Gore Family Memorial Foundation Trust

This foundation provides scholarships for undergraduate and graduate handicapped students enrolled in any field of study. Awards are based on financial need. Contact the Gore Family Memorial Foundation Trust, 230 S.E. First Ave., Fort Lauderdale, FL 33301.

National Federation of the Blind

This organization provides scholarships to blind students enrolled in undergraduate and graduate programs. Contact the National Federation of the Blind, 814 Fourth Ave., Grinnel, IA 50112.

Quota International Fellowship Fund

This group awards fellowships to graduate and undergraduate students who are either deaf or hearing impaired as well as to hearing students who intend to work with the deaf. Contact the Quota International Fellowship Fund, 1420 21st St., N.W., Washington, DC 20036.

FOR MORE INFORMATION

The following organizations can provide you with additional information on financial aid for students with disabilities.

Association on Handicapped Student Service Programs in Post-Secondary Education
P.O. Box 21192
Columbus, OH 43221

Council of Citizens with Low Vision
1400 Drake Rd.
Kalamazoo, MI 49007

Deafness and Communicative Disorders Branch
Switzer Bldg. MS 2312
Washington, DC 20202

Epilepsy Foundation
4251 Garden City Drive
Landover, MD 20785

Foundation for Science and the Handicapped
1141 Iroquois Drive
Napierville, IL 60540

Health Resources Center
One Dupont Circle, N.W.
Washington, DC 20036

Immune Deficiency Foundation
P.O. Box 586
Columbia, MD 21405

Helen Keller National Center
111 Middle Neck Rd.
Sands Point, NY 11050

Learning Disability Association
4156 Library Road
Pittsburgh, PA 15234

Lifecare Scholarship for the Respiratory Dependent
505 Central Ave.
Boulder, CO 80301

Ronnie Milsap Foundation
600 Renaissance Center
Detroit, MI 48234

National Association of the Deaf
814 Thayer Ave.
Silver Spring, MD 20910

National Federation of the Blind
1800 Johnson St.
Baltimore, MD 21320

National Information Center for Children
and Youth with Handicaps
1555 Wilson Blvd., Suite 508
Rosslyn, VA 22209

Office of Career Opportunities
National Technical Institute for the Deaf
One Lomb Memorial Drive
Rochester, NY 14623

U.S. Department of Education
Office of Special Education Programs
Office of Special Programs
400 Maryland Ave.
Washington, DC 20022

Recording for the Blind
20 Rozelle Rd.
Princeton, NJ 08540

Spina Bifida Association of America
1700 Rockville Pike
Rockville, MD 20852

United Cerebral Palsy Association
66 E. 34th St.
New York, NY 10016

WHAT'S NEXT

The federal government, state governments, and a number of private organizations and foundations give special priority to medicine and the health-related fields and administer many financial aid programs for students planning to enter those fields. We'll look at those special opportunities in chapter 13.

13

FINANCIAL AID FOR STUDENTS IN THE HEALTH PROFESSIONS

Because of the critical need for health care professionals in the United States, the federal government, state governments, and various organizations administer many financial aid programs exclusively for undergraduate and graduate student studying for degrees in the health professions. There are especially good opportunities for students interested in going into nursing, a field in which there are severe shortages in some parts of the country.

For the purpose of awarding financial aid, the government considers the following professions as being within the health care field: medicine, dentistry, nursing, osteopathic medicine, veterinary medicine, pharmacy, optometry, podiatric medicine, chiropractic education, clinical psychology, public health administration, occupational therapy, physical therapy, rehabilitation therapy, nutrition, social work, and allied health.

An education in a health care field is often more expensive than a traditional undergraduate education. If your child is interested in pursuing a health-related career, careful planning is required to make sure the costs can be met. In many cases, students who agree to work for a certain period of time in public health positions, the military, or in a geographic region where there's a shortage of health care professionals can have all or part of their educational costs covered.

FEDERALLY SPONSORED FINANCIAL AID PROGRAMS

The following federal programs provide financial assistance for undergraduates and graduate students in the health professions. The government considers students in nursing programs and pharmacy programs as undergraduates. Those in other health-related programs are generally considered graduate students. As with other federal programs, the funding and eligibility requirements for these programs may change from year to year.

Financial Assistance for Disadvantaged Health Professions Students Programs (FADHPS)

Students with a great deal of financial need who are enrolled in dental, medical, or osteopathy school are eligible for awards from this program. They must be U.S. citizens and come from a disadvantaged background as defined by guidelines set up by the U.S. Department of Health and Human Services. The awards can be used for tuition, fees, and living expenses and are available for all years of study. For more information, contact the Division of Student Assistance, Bureau of Health Professions, Health Resources and Services Administration, Parklawn Bldg., Room 8-48, 5600 Fishers Lane, Rockville, MD 20857.

Health Education Assistance Loan Program (HEAL)

This program provides financial aid to U.S. citizens or permanent residents who are enrolled full-time in approved schools. Applicants must demonstrate financial need and only use the loans for educational purposes. Students enrolled in schools of medicine, dentistry, osteopathy, optometry, podiatry, and veterinary medicine can borrow up to $20,000 a year for four years. Those studying other disciplines can borrow up to $12,500 a year for four years.

There is no federal interest subsidy for HEAL loans, and lenders have the option of offering a fixed or variable interest rate. Variable rates are tied to the 90-day Treasury bill plus 3.5 percent. Repayment can be as long as 25 years, and there is a deferment on repayment of principal while borrowers are completing residency or internship programs. Deferments also are considered for those serving with the Peace Corps, VISTA, the National Health Service Corps, or the military.

For more information about HEAL loans, write the Division of Student Assistance, HEAL Office, Bureau of Health Professions,

Health Resources and Services Administration, 5600 Fishers Lane, Rockville, MD 20857.

Health Professions Student Loan Program (HPSL)

This low-cost (5 percent), need-based program provides loans only to the neediest of students. Applicants must be U.S. citizens or permanent residents and enrolled in an approved school.

This program was first established with federal funds but now depends on payments from borrowers to fund new loans. As a result, the amount available for new loans changes from year to year. Students can borrow the cost of tuition and fees plus $2,500 each year. The awards are given by the financial aid offices of individual schools.

Repayment of HPSL loans doesn't start until a year after the borrower's graduation, and they don't begin to accrue interest until graduation. Borrowers can take up to 10 years for repayment. Students who continue on to more advanced training can obtain deferments, as can those who enter the Peace Corps, the U.S. Public Health Service, or the military. There are also loan forgiveness programs for graduates who go to work in designated areas where there are shortages of health professionals. For more information, contact the U.S. Department of Health and Human Services, Bureau of Health Personnel, Student and Institutional Assistance Branch, Parklawn Bldg., Room 9A-25, 5600 Fishers Lane, Rockville, MD 20857.

Loans for Disadvantaged Students Program

These are low-interest (5 percent), long-term loans for students in medicine, osteopathy, dentistry, optometry, pharmacy, podiatry, and veterinary medicine. Like Perkins Loans, the funds for these loans are allocated to individual colleges and are then distributed by their financial aid offices. The maximum amount that can be borrowed each year is $2,500.

Repayment begins a year after a student graduates and must be completed within 10 years. Students select either an equal payment or graduated payment option when they apply for the loans, and the minimum monthly payment is $15. As with the previous loans, there are conditions for deferment.

National Health Service Corps Loan Deferment Program

This program is kind of like the health care equivalent of ROTC or study in one of the service academies. It's a straight money-for-service trade that requires a big commitment on the part of students. Here's the deal: The National Health Service Corps will pay up to $25,000 for each of the first two years of a student's medical education and up to $35,000 for each subsequent year. In return, students agree to perform two years' service for each year of assistance, in an area of the country that has a shortage of health professionals. So a physician who uses the program to pay for each year of medical school will be expected to serve eight years, and that's after he or she completes an internship and a residency.

For more information on this program, contact the National Health Service Corps Repayment Program, 8201 Greensboro Drive, Suite 600, McLean, VA 22102. Phone 800-221-9393.

National Health Service Corps Scholarship Program

The National Health Service Corps also administers a scholarship program that provides awards to a limited number of students in medicine, dentistry, and osteopathy programs. The scholarship completely covers tuition, fees, and books and also provides a monthly living allowance. Scholarship recipients are required to serve one year with Health Service Corps for each year of support, or a minimum of two years, in an area of the country that has a shortage of health professionals. For more information, contact the National Health Service Corps Repayment Program, 8201 Greensboro Drive, Suite 600, McLean, VA 22102. Phone 800-221-9393.

Nursing Student Loan Program

Both part-time and full-time nursing students attending accredited schools can apply to this program for low-cost (6 percent) loans. Recipients must be U.S. citizens, nationals, or permanent residents. The program is set up like the HPSL program, with funds for new loans provided by repayments of older loans, so the amount of money available fluctuates from year to year. The awards are made by the financial aid directors of the schools. Students can borrow up to $2,500 a year for 4 years and have 10 years to repay the loan. Repayment starts 9 months after a student leaves school.

As with other health profession loans, there are deferment options for students who go on to graduate study or who serve in the military, the Peace Corps, or the U.S. Public Health Service.

For information, contact the Health Services Administration, Division of Student Assistance, Room 8-44, 5600 Fishers Lane, Rockville, MD 20857.

Scholarships for Disadvantaged Students Program.

This program provides financial assistance without any service or financial obligations on the part of the student. The program provides funds to severely needy and disadvantaged students pursuing degrees in nursing, medicine, osteopathy, and dentistry. Money for the program is provided to individual schools, and they are responsible for making the awards. The awards cover tuition, room and board, and other associated education costs. More information can be obtained from financial aid offices, or contact the Department of Health and Human Services, Public Health Service, Health Resources and Services Administration, Rockville, MD 20857.

Scholarship Program for Students with Exceptional Financial Need

This is a one-year only scholarship designed for needy students enrolled in medicine, dentistry, osteopathy, optometry, pharmacy, podiatry, and veterinary medicine. Funds are allocated by individual schools, and awardees are selected by the directors of financial aid. The value of each award can be up to the cost of tuition, books, and instruments. More information can be obtained from school financial aid directors.

MILITARY-SPONSORED FINANCIAL AID PROGRAMS

The armed forces sponsor several health professional financial aid programs that require military service after graduation.

Armed Forces Health Professions Scholarship Program

These scholarships cover tuition, books, and fees and also include a monthly living allowance. Recipients must serve in one branch of the armed services after graduation. Information can be obtained from school financial aid offices or by contacting the appropriate branch of the armed services:

U.S. Army
Army Medical Department Personnel
SGPE-PDM-S
1900 Half Street, S.W.
Washington, DC 20304-2000

U.S. Air Force
Recruiting Service
Director of Health Professionals Recruiting
Randolph Air Force Base
San Antonio, TX 78150

U.S. Navy/U.S. Marine Corps
Navy Recruiting Command
4015 Wilson Blvd.
Arlington, VA 22204

Reserve Officer Training Corps Nursing Scholarship Program

The Army, Navy, and Air Force ROTC programs provide scholarships to nursing students enrolled in colleges and universities with appropriate ROTC units. The scholarships completely cover tuition and fees and include a monthly allowance. Students are required to spend four years as commissioned officers after graduation. For information, contact:

U.S. Army ROTC
Army ROTC Scholarship Program
Fort Monroe, VA 23651

U.S. Air Force ROTC
Air Force ROTC Scholarship Program
Office of Public Affairs
Maxwell Air Force Base
Maxwell, AL 36112

U.S. Navy ROTC
Navy ROTC Scholarship Program
Information Center
P.O. Box 5000
Clifton, NJ 07015-9939

Uniformed Service University of the Health Sciences

This university is a medical school operated by the armed forces. Enrollment is limited and therefore very competitive. Tuition, fees, books, living expenses, and other educational costs are free, and students receive the salary of a lieutenant. For information, contact the Director of Admissions, Uniformed Service University of the Health Sciences, 4301 Jones Bridge Rd., Bethesda, MD 20841.

STATE-SPONSORED FINANCIAL ASSISTANCE PROGRAMS

The states also offer a variety of financial aid programs for health professions students. There are grant and scholarship programs, as well as low-cost, subsidized financial aid programs. For information on programs offered by individual states, contact the state agencies listed in chapter 10.

FINANCIAL AID OPPORTUNITIES FOR NURSING STUDENTS

The United States is currently suffering from a shortage of nurses. The problem is particularly severe in certain geographic regions of the country. There is also concern that the increased need for nurses caused by our rapidly growing elderly population will not be met. For these reasons, there are many financial aid opportunities for students interested in pursuing nursing as a profession.

Here are just a few of the opportunities that are available.

American Nurses Association Baccalaureate Scholarship Program

Minorities who are pursuing baccalaureate degrees in nursing are eligible for these awards. Contact the American Nurses Association, 1030 15th St., N.W., Washington, DC 20005.

Foundation of the National Student Nurses Association Scholarship Programs

This organization offers scholarship and loan programs to students enrolled or accepted for enrollment in nursing programs.

Contact the Foundation of the National Student Nurses Association, 555 W. 57th St., New York, NY 10019.

Knights Templar Loan Fund

This organization makes loans to qualified health professions students. Contact the Knights Templar Foundation, 14 E. Jackson Blvd., Suite 1700, Chicago, IL 60604-2293.

National Society, Daughters of the American Revolution Medical Scholarship Fund

The DAR awards scholarships to students enrolled in accredited nursing schools. Applicants are evaluated for financial need, academic performance, and recommendations. Contact the Office of Committees, NSDAR Administration Bldg., 1776 D Street, N.W., Washington, DC 20006-5392.

Nurses' Educational Funds

These scholarships are awarded to students enrolled in advanced nursing degree programs. Contact the Nurses' Educational Funds, National Student Nurses Association, 555 W. 57th St., New York, NY 10019.

Teamsters Union Scholarship Fund

The Teamsters Union maintains a scholarship program for members' children who have been accepted by accredited health professions schools. Information can be obtained from any local Teamsters Union office.

Indian Health Service Health Professions Scholarship Program

Administered by the U.S. Department of Health and Human Services, this program provides scholarships for students enrolled in a variety of health professions study, including nursing. The scholarships provide full tuition and a monthly allowance. Recipients must agree to work for the Indian Health Service after graduation for one year for each year of assistance. Contact the Indian Health Service Health Professions Scholarship Program, 1101 Kermit Drive, Oaks Tower #810, Nashville, TN 37217.

Veterans Administration Health Professions Scholarship Program

The Veterans Administration awards scholarships to full-time nursing students enrolled in both undergraduate- and graduate-level nursing programs. The scholarships cover tuition and fees and also provide a cost-of-living allowance. Recipients are required to work for the Veterans Administration for at least two years after graduation. Contact the Veterans Administration Professional Scholarship Program, Veterans Administration, Washington, DC 20420. Phone 800-368-5896.

OTHER SOURCES OF INFORMATION

These organizations are good sources of information on scholarship, grant, and loan programs for students in various disciplines within the health care professions.

American Association of Colleges of Nursing
One Dupont Circle, N.W.
Suite 530
Washington, DC 20036
202-463-6930

American Association of Colleges of Osteopathic Medicine
6110 Executive Blvd.
Suite 405
Rockville, MD 20852
301-468-0990

American Association of Colleges of Pharmacy
1426 Prince St.
Alexandria, VA 22314
703-739-2330

American Association of Colleges of Podiatric Medicine
6110 Executive Blvd.
Suite 204
Rockville, MD 20852
301-984-9350

American Association of Dental Schools
1625 Massachusetts Ave., N.W.
Washington, DC 20036
202-667-9433

American Medical Student Association
1890 Preston White Drive
Reston, VA 22091
703-549-3864

American Medical Women's Association
801 North Fairfax St.
Suite 400
Alexandria, VA 22314
703-549-3864

American Nurses' Association
2420 Pershing Rd.
Kansas City, MO 64108
816-474-5720

American Public Health Association
1015 15th St., N.W.
Washington, DC 20005
202-789-5600

American Veterinary Medical Association
1522 K Street, N.W.
Suite 828
Washington, DC 20005
202-659-2040

Association of American Medical Colleges
2450 N Street, N.W.
Washington, DC 20037
202-828-0400

Association of Schools and Colleges of Optometry
6110 Executive Blvd.
Suite 514
Rockville, MD 20852
301-231-5944

Association of Schools of Public Health
1015 15th St., N.W.
Washington, DC 20005
202-842-4668

Bureau of Health Professions
Division of Student Assistance
Parklawn Bldg.
5600 Fishers Lane
Rockville, MD 20857
301-443-4776

Council on Chiropractic Education
3209 Ingersoll Ave.
Des Moines, IA 50312
515-255-2184

National Association of Advisors for the Health Professions
P.O. Box 5017
Station A
Champaign, IL 61820
217-344-6013

National Health Council, Inc.
622 Third Ave., 34th Floor
New York, NY 10017-6765

Ask for the publication *Two Hundred Ways to Put Your Talent to Work in the Health Field.*

National League for Nursing
10 Columbus Circle
New York, NY 10019
212-582-1022

Ask for their publication *Scholarships and Loans for Nursing Education.*

National Medical Association
1012 Tenth St., N.W.
Washington, DC 20001
202-347-1895

National Medical Fellowships, Inc.
254 W. 31st St.
New York, NY 10001
212-714-0933

National Science Foundation
1800 G Street, N.W.
Washington, DC 20550
Ask for the publication *A Selected List of Fellowship Opportunities and Aids to Advanced Education.*

National Student Nurses Association
555 W. 57th St.
Suite 1325
New York, NY 10019
212-581-2211

Public Health Service
Department of Health and Human Services
Parklawn Bldg.
5600 Fishers Lane
Rockville, MD 20857
301-443-3087
Ask for the publication *Profiles of Financial Assistance Programs.*

WHAT'S NEXT?

At the end of World War II, the federal government created the GI Bill to help pay for the college educations of tens of thousands of veterans returning home from Europe and the Pacific. Millions more have since taken advantage of the program to get college degrees.

Today the military still provides a variety of scholarships and financial aid for active duty personnel, veterans, and their dependents. In chapter 14 we'll look at some of the ways the military might help pay for your child's education.

14

MILITARY-SPONSORED FINANCIAL AID PROGRAMS

At the end of World War II, the United States Congress established the GI Bill to help provide college educations for military personnel who had served in the war. These men and women went on to create the greatest period of economic prosperity the nation has ever seen. In their spare time they also managed to create the biggest population explosion the country has ever seen. Today, those children—the baby boomers—are the ones scrambling to pay for college. You're probably one of them.

Well, if that's the case, and you're either in the service or were in the service, you'll be happy to learn that the military still provides a great deal of financial aid for both active duty and retired personnel, as well as their dependents. Whether you're on active duty, retired, or a veteran, the chances are good there are programs you can tap to help finance your child's college costs.

PROGRAMS FOR MILITARY PERSONNEL

All the branches of the military provide financial aid programs for active duty enlisted personnel and officers interested in pursuing a college degree. Most pay a generous portion, from 75 to 100 percent, of tuition costs. Information on financial aid programs for military personnel can be obtained from local recruiters or military base education officers. The following are selected financial aid programs from the various branches of the armed services.

U.S. Army

Army College Fund.

This program helps fund college tuition costs for personnel who are still on active duty. Participants contribute $100 a month to an education fund, and the army provides matching funds. The amount contributed is based on the individual's length of service.

Army Continuing Education Programs.

The Army maintains a continuing education program that allows active duty personnel to enroll in a variety of academic and nonacademic courses. The programs include a basic skills education program, an English as a second language program, a high school completion program, an advanced skills education program, and an apprenticeship skills program.

Army Emergency Relief Program.

This program provides scholarships and loans to the dependents of active duty Army personnel, as well as those who died or were disabled during their military service. The awards are based on financial need and academic merit. For information, contact the U.S. Army Emergency Relief Program, 200 Stovall St., Alexandria, VA 22332.

Army Nurse Corps ROTC.

Nursing students who are interested in military service can participate in Army ROTC programs at selected colleges and qualify for ROTC tuition assistance. After graduation, they are commissioned as second lieutenants.

Federal Loan Repayment Program.

Active duty and reserve Army personnel who enlist in specially designated areas of training can qualify to have their Stafford and Perkins Student Loans paid by the army.

Opportunity Colleges Program.

This program is designed to allow Army personnel who may be periodically reassigned to different parts of the country to continue work on a college degree as they move. A network of junior colleges, community colleges, and four-year colleges allows for the transfer of credits and offers flexible course hours and admissions requirements.

U.S. Air Force

Air Force Aid Society.

This program offers subsidized loans to the children of qualified, active duty Air Force personnel. Applicants must be enrolled full-time at an approved school. For information, contact the Air Force Aid Society, National Headquarters, 1735 North Lynn St., Arlington, VA 22209.

The Community College of the Air Force.

This program offers active duty Air Force personnel the opportunity to earn an associate degree in applied science.

Operation Bookstrap.

This program offers career Air Force personnel the opportunity to attend accredited colleges and universities while they're on active duty.

U.S. Navy

Broadened Opportunity for Officer Selection and Training Program (BOOST).

High school seniors who have good grades but insufficient SAT scores to qualify for the Navy's ROTC scholarship program can enroll in BOOST, a training program designed to help them improve their scores. Those who graduate from the program are granted four-year ROTC scholarships at one of the Navy ROTC's participating colleges or universities. A few receive appointments to the U.S. Naval Academy.

Navy Supplemental Assistance Program.

This program offers grants and interest-free loans to qualified active members of the Navy or Marine Corps. Recipients must demonstrate financial need and have the recommendation of their commanding officer. Contact the Navy Relief Society Education Program, 801 N. Randolph St., Suite 1228, Arlington, VA 22203-1989.

Program for Surviving Children of Deceased While on Active Duty (CDAD).

This program provides financial aid for the children of Navy personnel who died while on active duty. Contact the Navy Relief Society Education Program, 801 N. Randolph St., Suite 1228, Arlington, VA 22203-1989.

Dependent's Scholarship Program.

This program provides scholarships to the children of Navy, Marine, and Coast Guard personnel enrolled full-time in accredited colleges and universities. Contact the Naval Military Personnel Command, Department of the Navy, Washington, DC 20370-5121.

Navy Federal Credit Union Students Loans.

The Navy's credit union offers federal Stafford Loans and Parent Loans for Undergraduate Students (PLUS) to Navy personnel who qualify for these programs. Contact the Navy Federal Credit Union, Security Place, P.O. Box 3350, Merrifield, VA 22119-3350.

Navy Relief Society.

This organization provides both undergraduate and graduate school loans to the children of active, retired, and reserve Navy and Marine Corps personnel. Contact the Navy Relief Society, 801 N. Randolph St., Suite 1228, Arlington, VA 22203-1989.

U.S. Marine Corps

Second Marine Division Association Memorial Scholarship Fund.

This fund was established to provide financial assistance to the children of Marines in the Second Marine Division who became disabled or were killed during active duty. Contact the Second Marine Division Association Memorial Scholarship Fund, P.O. Box 734, Wildwood, NJ 08260.

Marine Continuing Education Programs.

These programs support Marines who want to begin or continue their college educations. Participating personnel contribute from $25 to $100 a month to an education fund, and the money is matched two for one by the federal government. The Marine Corps Tuition Assistance Program will pay participants up to 75 percent of the cost of undergraduate courses and 90 percent of the cost of job-related courses.

Marine Corps Scholarship Foundation.

This foundation awards scholarships to the children of active, retired, and reserve Marines. Contact the Marine Corps Scholarship Foundation, P.O. Box 3008, Princeton, NJ 08540–3008.

PROGRAMS FOR VETERANS

Veterans' Educational Assistance Program (VEAP)

Military personnel who joined a branch of the armed forces between January 1, 1977 and July 1, 1985 qualify for this program. Participants can contribute from $25 to $100 a month to an education fund, and the government will match the contribution two to one.

Montgomery GI Bill

This program is available to all military personnel who joined the service after June 30, 1985. Paticipants receive $275 a month after two years of service and $350 a month after three years of service for their education funds.

PROGRAMS FOR CHILDREN AND DEPENDENTS OF VETERANS

American Legion Auxiliary National President's Scholarship Program

This organization awards scholarships every year to the children of veterans. Information on this program can be obtained from any local American Legion unit.

Air Force Sergeants Association Scholarship Program

The dependent children of veterans who served in the Air Force, Air National Guard, or Air Force Reserves are eligible for scholarships from this organization. The awards are based on financial need and academic excellence. Contact the Air Force Sergeants Association Scholarship Program, P.O. Box 50, Temple Hills, MD 20748-0050.

AMVETS National Memorial Scholarship Program

This program awards scholarships to high school seniors planning on attending both two- and four-year colleges, as well as students who have graduated from two-year colleges and are enrolling at four-year colleges to obtain a bachelor's degree. Recipients must demonstrate financial need and academic accomplishment. Contact AMVETS National Service Headquarters, 4647 Forbes Blvd., Lanham, MD 20706-9961.

Daughters of the Cincinnati Scholarship Program

The children of commissioned officers in the Army, Air Force, Marines, Navy, and Coast Guard are eligible for scholarships from this organization. Contact the Daughters of the Cincinnati Scholarship Program, Scholarship Administrator, 122 E. 58th St., New York, NY 10022.

Disabled American Veterans Scholarship Program

The children of veterans who suffered active duty disabilities can apply for scholarship assistance from this program. Applicants must demonstrate financial need and academic excellence. Contact the Scholarship Program, Disabled American Veterans, P.O. Box 4301, Cincinnati, OH 45250–0301.

Federal Benefits Veterans Administration Dependents Education Assistance Act

The children and spouses of veterans who were killed or totally disabled as a result of service-related injuries qualify for federal financial assistance. Children must be between the ages of 18 and 26. Contact the Division of Student Services and Veterans Programs, 400 Maryland Ave., S.W., Room 4010, Washington, DC 20202.

Knights of Columbus Educational Trust Fund

The Knights of Columbus also provide financial assistance to the children of veterans who were killed or disabled as a result of service-related injuries. Contact the Director of Scholarship Aid, Knights of Columbus, P.O. 1670, New Haven, CT 06507.

Noncommissioned Officers Association Scholarship Foundation

The children of noncommissioned officers who are members of this association are eligible for scholarships. Contact the NCOA Scholarship Foundation, P.O. Box 33610, San Antonio, TX 78265.

Retired Officers Association Scholarship Loan Program

This association offers financial assistance to the children of both active duty and retired members of the armed services. Contact the ROA Scholarship Loan Program, 201 North Washington St., Alexandria, VA 22314-2529.

FOR MORE INFORMATION

The following publications will provide additional information on financial aid programs for military personnel and their dependents.

- *Federal Benefits for Veterans and Dependents,* Veterans Administration, Government Printing Office, Washington, DC 20402.
- *How the Military Will Help You Pay for College: The High School Student's Guide to ROTC, the Academies, and Special Programs* by Don Betterton, Peterson's Guides, P.O. Box 2123, Princeton, NJ 80543-2123.
- *Financial Aid for Veterans, Military Personnel, and their Dependents,* Reference Service Press, 1100 Industrial Road, Suite 9, San Carlos, CA 94070.

WHAT'S NEXT?

Remember that 6' 6" point guard I mentioned in chapter 10? If he's currently living in the bedroom down the hall from you, you're a very fortunate person. You probably have basketball coaches practically camping on your doorstep. While other parents are frantically diving into every financial nook and cranny trying to come up with college tuition, your biggest problem is going to be making sure you can get good seats for the NCAA play-offs next March. With any luck, your son or daughter will be playing in them.

Athletic scholarships are a wonderful way to pay for college. They're hard to come by, but if you have a child with legitimate talent in a game that he or she loves, a scholarship might not be out of the question. We'll look at athletic scholarships in chapter 15.

15

ATHLETIC SCHOLARSHIPS

Winning an athletic scholarship to college is the dream of every high school athlete. Unfortunately, it's extremely hard to do. There are just a lot more athletes than there are scholarships, and only the best athletes are able to move on to collegiate competition.

It's a process that starts long before college. If your child plays sports, you've experienced the winnowing out process that occurs as kids grow older and move into higher levels of competition. There are fewer and fewer openings at each new level, and the less talented fall behind.

I've seen this with my own son. He's been playing ice hockey since he was 6 and is now, at 16, a junior playing his second year on the high school varsity. He came up through our local youth hockey association, moving from "house" teams, the least competitive level in which local teams play one another, to "travel" teams, which are composed of the best players in each age group who play teams from towns two and three hours away. The tryouts that preceded each move upward were nerve-wracking for him, and he watched several friends remain behind as he jumped to the next level. When he made the varsity last year, he reached a goal he had been eyeing since he started playing 10 years ago.

Although he doesn't talk about it, I know he wonders if he'll be good enough to play in college. Statistically, the odds are against him. The step from high school to college athletics is a big one, and for most high school athletes, graduation marks the end of varsity sports. The limited number of positions available on college teams ensures that only the most talented athletes move on. And of those, only the very best, the absolute cream of the crop, will be lucky enough to get athletic scholarships.

IS IT ATHLETICS OR BUSINESS?

This has become the perennial question about college athletics. Are these supremely talented athletes legitimate students, or are they just hired guns recruited to fill 100,000-seat stadiums and attract lucrative television contracts and bowl game invitations? Colleges and universities staunchly defend their programs, arguing that student-athletes are their most precious commodities and that providing them with a top-notch education will always be job one. At a lot of schools, this is true. Many manage to successfully combine varsity athletics and academics and produce graduates who are ready to go on to productive lives and careers.

But make no mistake about it. At its highest levels, college sports—particularly football and basketball—is a business, and a big one. The amount of money generated each year by a top twenty football program like that of Michigan or Notre Dame or Florida State can run into the tens of millions of dollars. Television contracts, ticket sales, licensing agreements with apparel manufacturers, bowl game appearance fees, and other sources of income make these programs cash cows for their schools and athletic departments. Do administrators mind doling out a few dozen scholarships to help bring in the money? Not at all. It's just a cost of doing business, thank you very much.

It's such an obvious business, in fact, that its most severe critics say that colleges should pay the athletes over and above the value of the scholarships they already receive. The athletes generate the money, the critics say, so let them share in the wealth. This will never happen, of course, but it does serve to illustrate just how much money is involved.

THE GRADUATION ISSUE

One reason college sports, particularly big-time football and basketball programs, receive so much negative publicity is the often dismal graduation record of their athletes. A 1994 study discovered that 29 percent of Division I men's basketball programs—that's 87 colleges and universities—hadn't graduated a single athlete who had entered their schools as freshman recruits six years earlier. This provides further ammunition to those who argue that some universities use their athletes to make money and then spit them out when they've outlived their usefulness.

Part of the problem has always been the admission of athletes who have no business walking through the gates of a university in the first place. They're more than ready for the athletics, they're just not ready for the academics. Many go from high school to junior colleges or prep schools for a year or two to get their grades in good enough shape to be admitted to college. But the graduation rates make it obvious that many of them will never leave with a sheepskin.

The NCAA's academic requirements for college eligibility have been toughened in recent years, although they're still quite lenient. We'll take a look at them later in the chapter.

THE COLLEGE SPORTS HIERARCHY

Almost all the athletic programs at America's colleges and universities fall into one of four categories. Three are governed by the National Collegiate Athletic Association (NCAA). The fourth is the realm of the National Association of Intercollegiate Athletics (NAIA).

There also are several smaller organizations whose member schools may also belong to the NCAA or NAIA. They include the National Christian College Athletic Association (NCCAA), the National Bible College Athletic Association (NBCAA), and the National Little College Athletic Association (NLCAA).

NCAA Division I

The 302 schools in the NCAA's Division I are the nation's biggest—the state universities and the larger private institutions. They're the schools you see competing in nationally televised football games in the fall and in basketball games in the winter. They're Ohio State, Alabama, UCLA, Syracuse, Nebraska, and all the other names that come to mind when you think of the nation's best teams. It's not just coincidence. Division I teams offer the most athletic scholarships of all the NCAA divisions.

According to NCAA guidelines, Division I schools must compete at the highest level possible in football, basketball, or both. They must play primarily other Division I schools and compete on a regional or national level. Their football stadiums have to seat at least 30,000 people, and they must average at least 17,000 per game. All told, Division I schools must field a minimum of seven teams each for men and women. Each team must compete in a minimum number of contests each year.

The NCAA divides its Division I schools in football. The top 104 football schools are classified as Division I-A. All the other schools that have football teams fall into Division I-AA. Some of the teams in this category are former Division II powerhouses whose programs have moved so far ahead that they became much better than the rest of Division II but not quite competitive with the Penn States and Notre Dames of the world. The rest are weaker Division I programs—the Ivy League teams, for example—that also aren't competitive against Division I-A teams.

One of the great things about Division I-AA is that it has a play-off system at the end of the year to determine a national champion. There are many frustrated sports fans (and coaches) hoping and praying that the powers-that-be in Division I-A will eventually figure out how to do the same.

NCAA Division II

The schools in Division II are usually a step down in size from Division I schools and offer fewer scholarships. They must have a minimum of four varsity sports each for men and women and compete against both Division I and Division II schools.

NCAA Division III

Division III schools are not permitted to offer athletic scholarships; all their financial aid to athletes is strictly need-based. Among Division III schools are many of the nation's best small colleges with first-class academic programs and decades-old athletic rivalries. They also are required to field at least four varsity teams for both men and women, and their football and basketball teams must play at least half their games against other Division III schools.

NAIA

The 400 or so schools in the NAIA are smaller schools, although technically the association is open to any four-year college, and some schools are members of both the NAIA and the NCAA. Member schools are organized into districts, and there are two levels of competition in football and basketball but one level for everything else. Most of the schools in the NAIA offer a limited number of scholarships.

WHO PLAYS WHAT?

The NCAA divisional structure is based primarily on strength in football and basketball. But among less popular sports, the national powers frequently come from the lower divisions. This is because the NCAA allows all member schools to play one sport (other than football and basketball) in a higher division.

A good example is ice hockey. For obvious reasons, the sport has its American roots in the Northeast and upper Midwest, and many of the country's best teams—North Dakota, Lake Superior State, Clarkson, Ferris State, St. Lawrence, Colorado College—come from small Division II and Division III schools in those regions. For ice hockey purposes, however, they're classified as Division I. This pattern also occurs in other sports such as wrestling, lacrosse, men's and women's soccer, and even baseball and golf.

Schools can also play down a division in one sport, provided their program meets the scholarship requirements of the lower division.

WHERE ARE THE SCHOLARSHIPS?

Predictably, the formula for doling out athletic scholarships is often complicated. (As you get to know it, you'll discover that there's a lot about the NCAA that's complicated.) The main reason is that they can be full scholarships or partial scholarships. A full scholarship goes to one athlete. But a partial scholarship can be divided up among many athletes.

For example, Division I baseball teams have 11.7 scholarships to distribute among the members of their teams every year. But they can be distributed as partial scholarships. Let's say a coach decides to carry a roster of 21 players. He may choose to divide the 11.7 scholarships up equally, in which case each player would get 0.557 of a scholarship (this stuff must drive the bursar's office nuts). Or he could choose to award 5 full scholarships and divide the rest up equally among the remaining 15 players. He could also choose any number of other ways to divide up the scholarships.

Here are all the NCAA-sanctioned sports for which scholarships can be awarded. Not all sports are played at all colleges, however, and not all colleges offer scholarships in all the sports in which they do participate.

- archery
- badminton
- baseball
- basketball
- bowling
- crew
- cross-country
- fencing
- field hockey
- football
- golf
- gymnastics
- ice hockey
- lacrosse
- riflery
- skiing
- soccer
- softball
- squash
- swimming and diving
- synchronized swimming
- team handball
- tennis
- track and field
- volleyball
- water polo
- wrestling

NCAA Division I

Division I has both full and partial scholarships. In Division I-A football, however, all awards must be full scholarships. Teams can have as many as 85 players with scholarships and give out 25 new scholarships a year. Division I-AA schools, on the other hand, can award partial football scholarships. They are allowed to field the equivalent of 63 full scholarship players, and they can award the equivalent of 30 full scholarships a year.

Division I basketball programs also must award only full scholarships, 13 a year for men's teams and 15 for women's teams. Other Division I sports dole out varying numbers of scholarships, both full and partial, depending on the number of members required to field a team.

Take note that the Ivy League, although Division I, does not award athletic scholarships. All its awards are based on financial need. If you have a scholar-athlete who wants to attend an Ivy League school, go back and read chapter 9 again. It's time to get poor.

NCAA Division II

The biggest differences between Division I and Division II are that fewer scholarships are awarded, and partial scholarships can be awarded in all sports. In football, for instance, a team can award 36 equivalent scholarships every year.

NCAA Division III

Division III schools do not award athletic scholarships. However, there is no limit on the number of athletes that can receive need-based grants.

NAIA

The NAIA has no limits on the number of athletic scholarships a school can award. However, since most schools in this association are small and have limited financial resources, the number of athletic scholarships available is quite limited.

WHAT'S THE DURATION OF ATHLETIC SCHOLARSHIPS?

Once upon a time, the dream of every high school athlete was to get a "full ride" to good old State U. Four or five years of girls, guts, and glory, and it would all be paid for.

Things are a little more strict these days. You can still get the four- or five-year scholarship, but now it has to be renewed every year. And renewal is not automatic. It may require a review by a committee of athletic department administrators. The scholarships of athletes who become injured or ill must also be considered for renewal. And there are no guarantees that a school will be particularly sympathetic to someone who may no longer be able to compete. The school may decide that the scholarship can be better invested in someone who has a healthy body to put out on the field. It's a tough call, but that's life. Athletes who do have their scholarships canceled or reduced do have the option of appealing the school's decision.

ACADEMIC REQUIREMENTS

NCAA

Faced with enormous criticism over its lenient admissions policies, the NCAA has slowly been making them more stringent in recent years.

To qualify for athletic scholarships at Division I and Division II schools, a student must graduate from high school with a minimum 2.0 GPA in a core curriculum that includes at least 13 academic courses. These must include three units of English (four in Division I); two units of math; two units of social science; two units of natural or physical science; and four additional units selected from among courses in math, social science, natural or physical science, foreign language, computer science, philosophy, or religion.

Division I eligibility is also based on a combination of high school GPA, SAT scores, and ACT scores. The lowest acceptable GPA for admission is 2.0. At that level, the minimum acceptable SAT score is 1020, and the minimum acceptable ACT score is 21. As a student's GPA rises, the minimum SAT and ACT scores become lower. The following chart shows the requirements for 1997–98.

High School GPA	*Minimum SAT*	*Minimum ACT*
2.500 or higher	820	17
2.475	830	18
2.450	840	18
2.425	850	18
2.400	860	18
2.375	870	18

High School GPA	*Minimum SAT*	*Minimum ACT*
2.350	880	19
2.325	890	19
2.300	900	19
2.275	910	19
2.250	920	19
2.225	930	20
2.200	940	20
2.175	950	20
2.150	960	20
2.125	970	20
2.100	980	21
2.075	990	21
2.050	1000	21
2.025	1010	21
2.000	1020	21

These rules don't apply to Division III schools. Requirements for need-based financial aid at Division III schools are set by the schools themselves, their conferences, and the NCAA.

NAIA

Freshmen at NAIA schools must meet two of the following three criteria to participate in a sport (and therefore to qualify for a scholarship): They must graduate in the top half of their high school class, have a GPA of at least 2.0, or score a minimum of 860 on their SATs or 18 on their ACTs. Students who don't meet these requirements are not permitted to play a sport until their sophomore year.

WHO CAN OR CAN'T PLAY?

There are several situations that will prevent an athlete from participating in some or all college athletics. Here are two that will make an athlete completely ineligible for all sports.

- The athlete agrees to general representation (as opposed to representation in just one sport) by an agent or some other entity that will market him as an athlete.
- If, after participating in a college sport, the athlete permits

or accepts payment for the use of his name or image in advertising or promoting the sale of a product or service.

One of the most ridiculous blowups in NCAA history occurred over this issue after the 1996 NCAA basketball championship game. T-shirts appeared for sale printed with an image of members of the winning team, the University of Kentucky, celebrating on the court moments after the game had ended. The image showed only senior players, so there was no concern about anyone losing their eligibility. But then someone noticed—in the background, out of focus, and almost completely blocked from view by another player's shoulder—a portion of the face of an underclassman on the team. The NCAA practically went into hysterics, and the poor player almost lost his scholarship.

These situations will make an athlete ineligible for a particular sport.

• The athlete has signed a professional contract, asked to be made eligible for a professional draft, played on a professional team, or been paid or promised payment in that sport.
• The athlete tried out for a professional team in that sport while still in college.
• The athlete agreed to be represented in that sport by an agent or other entity.

If an athlete has played professionally in one sport, he can still play at the collegiate level in another. However, if he's under contract or being paid by a professional team while in college, he cannot receive a scholarship to play another sport. But if he ends the relationship with the professional team, his eligibility is restored.

He can also play if, prior to entering college, he tried out for a professional team and received expense money for the tryout (this is common in baseball, for example) or he was a paid instructor in a sport.

DECIDING WHERE TO PLAY

Every high school athlete dreams of playing at the very top level in college. Is there a running back anywhere in the country who hasn't fantasized at least once about scoring the winning touchdown in the Orange Bowl for the national championship? Can any basketball player say he or she never sat in front of the television watching the NCAA Final Four and not pictured themselves on the court?

Dreaming is only natural. But when it comes time to consider a college program, it'll be time for a reality check. Here's the main question.

Big Time or Small Time?

Although everyone dreams of the big time, only the very best players will make it to Division I schools. An important part of seeking a college athletic scholarship is matching talents to the proper level of competition. If you have a son who's a reasonably talented high school quarterback but is not particularly big or fast, he would probably be quite comfortable at a Division II or Division III school. If he's the second coming of Dan Marino, then you can consider Division I.

Another misconception many athletes have is that they're going to make it to the pros. So they convince themselves they need to play Division I. In reality, the odds of a high school football player reaching the pros are about 6,000 to one. For a high school basketball player, the odds are about 10,000 to one.

I've been involved in sports all my life, and I've only known two people who made it to the professional level. Both were football players. One is Joe Italiano, a friend of mine from high school who played offensive tackle at the University of Pennsylvania and then had a brief professional career with the Memphis Southmen in the short-lived World Football League in the mid-70s. The other is Lydell Mitchell, a running back on a rival high school team who became a star at Penn State and then enjoyed a successful professional career with the Baltimore Colts and San Diego Chargers. If you follow football, you'll remember Lydell. It's unlikely you'll remember Joe.

These two achieved their success because they possessed the unique combination of size, speed, skill, and attitude that's necessary for a career in big-time athletics. But these attributes were quite evident by the time they were 14 or 15. Lydell was bigger than just about everyone on the field and was virtually impossible to tackle one-on-one or to catch at all once he got in the open field. Joe is 6'3" and weighed close to 225 by the time he left high school. As a pro, he weighed around 275. He was also extremely motivated.

The point I'm making is that in my experience the kind of talent that takes people to the top levels in athletics is evident fairly early on. Granted, there is the occasional Michael Jordan, who didn't make his high school basketball team until his junior year. But in most cases, if a child has the talent to play at the top it will be evident by 9th or 10th grade. They're simply much better than everyone else.

Make sure you and your child are realistic in your expectations. Everyone wants to be the next Emmitt Smith or Scottie Pippen, but most will be fortunate just to be able to participate in college sports. Be honest about the level of competition your child can play at, and make that your goal. Reaching high is noble. But reaching too high can only lead to disappointment.

THE RECRUITING GAME

While college and university athletic teams are busy competing on the playing field, flocks of college scouts are beating the bushes for the high school athletes who will fill their rosters two, three, and four years down the line. The best athletes are usually easy to find. But there are also thousands of athletes who either haven't quite hit their stride yet or somehow have simply escaped attention. Those athletes are equally important to scouts, and sometimes they have to take it upon themselves to make sure the scouts find them.

GETTING NOTICED

If a high school athlete is good enough, he or she won't have to worry about getting noticed. Colleges and universities have sophisticated scouting programs designed to weed out the best athletes in the nation, no matter how far off the beaten track they might be. Some particularly exceptional athletes begin to get tracked by 8th or 9th grade. By the time they're juniors and seniors, coaches and their representatives are practically camped outside their homes. They'll be able to pick and choose from any number of scholarship offers.

It can get ridiculous. There have been cases where highly prized athletes have received several pieces of mail from a college or university every day for months on end, including personal letters from coaches, administrators, and current players. The coaches and their representatives will visit the home, hoping to win over the parents, as well as the athletes. The athletes get calls from prominent alumni telling them what a wonderful opportunity it is to attend such a great school. Sometimes all the attention of the coaches and their entourages ends up undermining their own efforts. They become such annoyances that they end up driving the athletes to other schools.

That kind of attention only goes to the most elite athletes, however. Others need to do a little self-promotion to make sure they get noticed.

The Parents' Role

It's often difficult being the parent of a high school athlete. Not only are the athletes dealing with the demands of their sport but they're also working hard to keep up with their academics. They're also confronting the many confusing issues that accompany adolescence. For a parent, there's a fine line between being supportive and being pushy, and knowing when you're crossing that line is not always easy. It's a common cause of tension between high school athletes and their parents.

Still, there are many things a parent can do to help a child obtain a scholarship. As I mentioned earlier in the book, the search for scholarships, grants, and other forms of financial aid should start early. By the time your child is a sophomore, the two of you should be well into your search, evaluating schools for their match to your child's athletic skills and academic interests.

One of your child's responsibilities will be to contact schools that have the programs he or she is interested in to get more information. You can certainly assist in this phase of the project. Your assistance will also be needed in helping your child weigh different offers and making plans to cover any costs that may not be covered by a scholarship.

What you don't want to do is become too demanding and force your child into a situation he or she doesn't want. There are countless horror stories about kids who are brought up by their parents to become star athletes. Sometimes the talent is there. Sometimes it isn't. But regardless of the talent level, the parents are unrelenting in their pressure to get their kids to perform up to a real—or perceived—level of ability.

The results can be disastrous. About 20 years ago, I knew a young man whose father was convinced his son was going to play at the top level of Division I basketball and then go to the NBA. The kid was a decent player with some skills, but anyone who knew anything about the game knew he'd play at a Division III college at best. As for the NBA? There was no way. He was just too small and too slow.

But his father couldn't see it. He put enormous pressure on his son, to the point of showing up at practices and then critiquing his performance on the drive home. During games, the man would lose it completely and scream at his son, at the boy's coach, and even at the referees. Finally, after he let loose a particularly nasty string of epithets against a referee one night he was banned permanently by the school's athletic director from attending games, both home and away.

For his son, it was a liberating experience, at least at first. He was more relaxed, and his performance improved markedly. But then his father pulled him out of school, enrolled him in a nearby private school, and started the same nonsense all over again. By the time his son was a senior, he had given up basketball altogether, and his relationship with his father was in tatters. Today they have very little contact with each other.

The Guidance Counselor's Role

You and your child must remember that a college's academic programs are as important as its athletic programs. Your child is a scholar-athlete, and you'll notice that the term scholar comes first in that phrase. A guidance counselor can help you and your child wade through the academic questions you'll have about your candidate colleges.

A guidance counselor can also help the two of you interpret the sometimes confusing academic requirements the NCAA has for athletes who are awarded college scholarships (later in the chapter we'll see what can happen when those requirements aren't met). That person will also be responsible for forwarding your child's academic transcripts to interested colleges.

The Coach's Role

High school coaches can be a valuable resource in helping an athlete prepare for the transition to college athletics. First of all, a good coach will give an athlete an honest assessment of his or her skills and point him or her to the proper level of college competition. A coach can help an athlete prepare letters to colleges expressing interest in their programs. Many coaches have extensive networks they can use to get the word out about a player. A coach can also talk with college coaches to see if an athlete's size and skills will mesh with the college's program.

The Athlete's Role

Despite the assistance of parents and coaches, the bulk of the responsibility of pursuing a college scholarship belongs to the athlete. The first step is deciding what colleges have the athletic and academic programs that match up to their interests and skills.

Once that has been accomplished, the lines of communication need to be established. During the sophomore year, an athlete should start making preliminary inquires to the colleges on the list. Letters to coaches expressing interest in their programs will usually result in some brochures and other material from both athletic departments and admissions offices.

During the junior year, an athlete will begin to narrow the list of schools and send out another round of letters to coaches expressing a serious interest in the school. This time, though, the letter should include a resume of athletic accomplishments, a letter of recommendation from the high school coach, and transcripts. Videos are also a good way for a coach to see an athlete in action. However, they should be short and tightly edited so there's no extraneous footage on them.

The real work begins during the senior year. NCAA rules prohibit college coaches from phoning or having direct contact with recruits until after their junior year. Up to that point, about all a coach can do is write to athletes.

During the senior year, however, an athlete can visit schools and meet with coaches personally, but only after they've supplied the school with the scores from their PSATs, SATs, or ACTs.

There are numerous rules governing visits. If an athlete is paying the tab, he or she can visit a school an unlimited number of times. If the school is paying for the visit, only one visit is permitted. And overall, only five paid visits to Division I and Division II schools are permitted. There are also periods when candidates are not allowed to visit with coaches.

This is the period when athletes need to learn as much about a school's athletic program as possible. They should make a list with all the questions they can think of. Talking to other athletes is a good way to get inside information on what the program is really like. They also should get out of the athletic environment and spend time visiting the rest of the campus and talking to other students. Once the visits are over and all the questions are asked, the athlete and the school will know whether they're right for each other.

Watch Out for Scouting Services

Many promising high school athletes will be contacted by scouting services who claim they can help them land scholarships. Some may ask for a fee based on the amount of the scholarship the athlete receives. The NCAA does not sanction or endorse these services, and it prohibits them from charging a scholarship-based fee. Check with the NCAA if your child should be contacted by such a service to make sure that it doesn't jeopardize your child's eligibility.

KNOW THE RULES

This is the most important piece of advice I can give any high school scholar-athlete who hopes to earn a college scholarship. The NCAA is a minefield of arcane rules and regulations, and it's important that you know them before you start the scholarship search.

Consider the story of poor Winny Brodt, a high school ice hockey player from a suburb of Minneapolis. She was an honor role student in high school, a member of the National Honor Society, and had a 3.5 GPA. These impressive academic achievements and her hockey skills won her a scholarship to play hockey at the University of New Hampshire beginning in the fall of 1996.

Then the NCAA struck. While Winny was still at home packing for New Hampshire, she was notified that she couldn't accept her scholarship. The reason? Among her 13 core courses was an English course that hadn't been certified by the NCAA's academic clearing house.

The course in question was considered an advanced course by Winny's high school. But the clearing house decided it was a reading skills enhancement course, and it turned down the school's request to have the course reclassified. Then the NCAA turned down Winny's request for a waiver. As a result, she spent what should have been her freshman year in college living at home and taking an English course at her old high school to qualify for the scholarship.

Winny wasn't the only student to be tripped up by NCAA rules in 1996. The NCAA estimates that as many as 1,500 students requested waivers. Most were over English courses that didn't meet standards (beginning in 1996 the NCAA began requiring four core English courses for students entering Division I schools rather than three). A large part of the problem is poor communication between the NCAA and high school guidance offices. Some schools seldom produce college-level athletes, and their guidance offices are unfamiliar with NCAA rules. In other schools the guidance counselors are so overworked it's almost impossible to keep up with the ever-changing NCAA requirements.

The lesson to be learned here is that you and your child need to do your own research on NCAA requirements for admission. Consult your guidance office, too. But if there are any areas you don't understand, go to the NCAA directly for clarification.

FOR MORE INFORMATION

Here are a few books that can help you and your child learn more about athletic scholarships.

- *Get Yourself a College Sports Scholarship* by Susan M. Wilson, Macmillan, New York, 1996.
- *How to Get an Athletic Scholarship: A Student-Athlete's Guide to Collegiate Athletics* by Whitney Minnis, ASI Publications, 1995.
- *The Road to Athletic Scholarships: What Every Student-Athlete, Parent & Coach Needs to Know* by Kim McQuilken, New York University Press, New York, 1996.

WHAT'S NEXT?

All the previous chapters in this book have examined strategies to come up with the money to pay for your child's college. But the one thing we haven't examined is how to cut down on college expenses. We'll look at how you can do this in chapter 16.

16

CUTTING COLLEGE COSTS

I have a little slogan that I'm fond of using when discussing strategies to reduce business costs, but it's just as appropriate for college costs.

"Cheap is good. Free is better."

In other words, I hate to spend money I don't have to spend. And when I do have to spend it, I try to spend as little as possible. That includes what I have to spend on college.

Keeping your child's college costs down means using every trick in the book. Unless you're very lucky, you're not going to be able to make college completely free. (Where's that point guard when you need him?) But you can do a lot to make it cheaper. Here are some of the best strategies.

COMMUTING

Having your child live at home and commute to college is one of the most obvious methods to save thousands of dollars a year. Many colleges and universities have large commuter enrollments. Most of them are state-supported schools, so their tuitions are reasonable, too.

Of course, the downside is that one of the great parts of going to college is living on campus and being part of everything that goes on there. Dorm life is something everybody should experience at least once.

STATE UNIVERSITIES

This is another fairly obvious strategy for the cost-conscious college shopper. Some large states, such as California, Pennsylvania, and New York, have equally large state university systems, and many of their colleges are highly thought of. The State University of New York's Binghamton University is routinely listed as one of the best buys in the country by college guides.

START AT A CHEAPER COLLEGE AND THEN TRANSFER

Want an Ivy League degree at a cut-rate price? A student who attends a state school, commuter college, or community college for two years and then transfers to a more expensive school can save thousands of dollars. And his sheepskin looks just the same as the kid who spent four years at the big bucks school.

BUY A RENTAL PROPERTY

Parents who can afford it find that buying a rental property for their child to live in is a great way to save on costs. The rent from their child's housemates is usually enough to cover the mortgage and then some, so their child's room and board costs are covered. Not only that, they enjoy any increase in the value of the property while they own it.

ADVANCED COURSES IN HIGH SCHOOL

Students who take advanced placement (AP) courses in high school can transfer those credits to their colleges and universities. More than 10,000 secondary schools offer AP courses, and 2,700 colleges will allow them to be applied to an undergraduate degree, provided a student's scores on the final exams are high enough.

There are also about [illegible]50 public and private high schools that offer two-year college preparatory curriculums that lead to an international baccalaureate (IB). Completion of the program qualifies a student for up to a year's credits at approximately 500 colleges and universities.

RESIDENT ADVISER POSITIONS

Many schools allow upperclassmen to serve as floor advisers or residence hall advisers in return for discounts on their room and board.

ACCELERATED PROGRAMS

A degree in three years can cut college costs by 25 percent. If you factor in the income the graduate earns during that fourth year, the savings can be more than 50 percent. Around 175 schools have established three-year undergraduate programs.

Needless to say, this strategy is not for everyone. Graduating in three years requires enormous course loads each semester. For kids who are going to be challenged by basic college work, it's out of the question. It also means less time for sports, socializing, and other activities. But if your whiz kid is organized, used to working hard, and can handle pressure, it can be a great way to save money.

COOPERATIVE EDUCATON PROGRAMS

Cooperative education programs allow students to alternate working full time and going to college full time. It generally takes at least five years to earn a degree under these programs. Although the federal government is the largest employer in these programs, they're not need-based, and independent businesses also participate. Employment can also be matched to a student's career interests.

SEND TWO FAMILY MEMBERS AT ONCE

This is the bulk discount approach to paying for college. Most schools will offer discounts to siblings or other family members of a student who is enrolled full time. Having more than one child in school at the same time will also usually increase the amount of financial aid a family qualifies for. As a result, many families decide to wait until two siblings who may only be a year or two apart both graduate from high school and then send them off to college together. If you don't have two kids who are that close in age, keep in mind that this is also an excellent opportunity for you or your spouse to go back to school.

CREDIT FOR "LIFE EXPERIENCES"

Some schools take the old saying ''Experience is the best teacher'' quite literally by awarding students credits for work, travel, or other experiences.

OFF-HOUR COURSES

Off-hour courses are offered at night, on weekends, and during summers and usually charge a lower rate than regularly scheduled courses. They also work well for students who have jobs or other responsibilities. Many students have earned every credit for their degrees attending these courses.

WORK OFF THE RENT

Some landlords will give students a discount on rent in return for a certain number of hours of work on their property each week.

THE PROS AND CONS OF PREPAID TUITION PLANS

One of the more creative approaches to financing a college education is paying tuition ahead of time, even though your child may be 5 or 10 or even 15 years away from college. As this book was being written nine states—Alabama, Alaska, Florida, Kentucky, Massachusetts, Michigan, Ohio, Pennsylvania, and Texas—had implemented prepaid tuition plans. Twenty-one other states had legislation pending to implement their own. Since these programs began in Michigan in the mid-80s, an estimated 500,000 families have bought contracts.

Prepaid tuition plans have both advocates and critics, and both sides make some good points. Let's take a look at some of their arguments.

How Do Prepaid Tuition Plans Work?

Prepaid tuition plans are the reverse of the old Buy Now, Pay Later approach to purchasing something. There are slight variations from state to state, but the basic idea is this: Rather than paying a higher tuition when your child enrolls in college, you lock in the average current tuition rate at the public institutions in your state by giving the money to the state while your child is growing up. When your child graduates from high school and does enroll, the state makes up the difference between the guaranteed tuition you already paid and the current average tuition at its state-supported institutions.

How does the state afford it? Simple. It invests the money you and other parents have given it and uses the earnings to cover the difference between the two amounts. If it earns more than that, the state makes a profit, since it's only guaranteeing you the cost of tuition when your child enrolls in college. So—in theory, anyway—everybody comes out ahead. The college gets its money, you pay less for tuition, and the state can possibly earn a profit.

The Advantages of Prepaid Tuition Plans

The biggest advantage of prepaid tuition plans is that they operate like forced savings plans. For some people, particularly those with poor money management habits, this is a benefit. They don't have to pay the money in one lump sum and can make weekly or monthly contributions. They can even have the money deducted from their paychecks so they never even see it and they're not tempted to spend it on something else. At that point, saving for college becomes something they really don't even have to worry about anymore. The money's being put away, and they know it will be there when they need it.

Another advantage to prepaid tuition plans is that the money put into the plan is tax deductible when your child redeems it to pay for tuition. It's also backed by the individual states, so there's virtually no chance you'll lose it.

If you're like most people, a couple of questions immediately come to mind. The first is, Are there limits on where my child can attend college? In most states the answer is no, your child can enroll in a variety of public and private institutions throughout the United States and the money will be applied to the tuition cost.

The second question is, What happens if my child doesn't get accepted or decides not to go to college? In that case you have two options. You can transfer the tuition credits to another family member for their education or you can receive a refund.

The Disadvantages of Prepaid Tuition Plans

The big argument against prepaid tuition plans is obvious. When examined from a purely economic perspective, they're a lousy investment. The rate of return on the money you give the state is limited to the increase in tuition between the time you invest the money and when you use it for college. In other words, if tuition rises an average of 5 percent annually during that time, that's your annual return on investment. Meanwhile, if the state has earned 15 percent annually with the investments it's made with your money, it's keeping the extra 10 percent as profit.

This would drive any experienced investor nuts. You should invest the money yourself they'll tell you, and they're right. People who invest in prepaid tuition plans are falling victim to their own weaknesses. If they can afford to put money into a prepayment plan, they should be able to have the discipline to put it into zero-coupon bonds, mutual funds, or retirement funds where it would earn a greater return. By giving it to the state, they're just letting someone else do their work for them and paying a big premium for the service.

Another problem is that some states guarantee to pay the existing tuition when your child enters college. Others only guarantee an estimated tuition that's determined at the outset of the plan. If the estimate is low, you're out of luck. And regardless of whether the agreed-upon tuition amount is current or estimated, it's the tuition at state institutions. That means if your child wants to attend a private college or university, you're going to have to come up with a lot more money. At that point, the money you lost by not doing your own investing will loom large indeed.

Yet another problem can arise when, for whatever reason, you seek a refund. You'll only get a very small portion of the interest the money has earned, and there may be ridiculous conditions attached to getting even that. In Florida, for instance, you'll only earn 5 percent on your money, and you'll only get that if your child wins a full scholarship, becomes disabled, or dies. Otherwise, you just get back the amount you put in, with no interest at all. If you've been socking money into that plan for 10 or 15 years, you're going to be extremely unhappy.

Make Your Own Decision

So are prepaid tuition plans a good idea? My personal opinion is they're a waste of time and money and play to people's weaknesses. With a little effort and self-discipline, you should be able to put the same money in investments where it will appreciate much faster than the increase in tuition.

At the same time, I will acknowledge that some people are financial idiots and will likely always be financial idiots. If it takes a plan like this to get them to put money aside for their children's education, it's better than not saving at all.

It's really up to you. An honest self-analysis will tell you whether or not you're the type of person who needs something like this. If you like the idea of a plan where your money is invested on a regular basis, that keeps your money basically untouchable until it's needed, and ties you into a cheaper deal when it's needed, prepaid tuition plans may be the ticket. But if you have confidence in your abilities to investigate investment opportunities and then steer money into them, I'd go the investment route.

STUDENT EMPLOYMENT PROGRAMS

Of course, the best way to knock some money off the cost of college is to let your child contribute by working part-time during the school year. That money, plus income earned during summer vacations, can make a pretty good dent in the bill. It's not unreasonable to expect your child to come up with $3,000 to $4,000 a year toward college and still have some spending money left over.

Where to Look

The federal government, the states, and colleges all provide employment opportunities for college students. In some cases, part-time jobs can be arranged in fields that match up with students' areas of interest. The student employment office of your child's college will have information on job opportunities.

Here are some of the major student employment programs.

Federal work-study program.

This is one of the nation's biggest work-study programs. It provides employment on- and off-campus for students who demonstrate financial need. Federal funds pay for 50 percent of a student's wages for non-college jobs and 70 percent of the wages for college jobs. There is a limit on how much a student can earn in this program, and the amount changes each year. The jobs are made part of the financial aid package and are administered by college financial aid offices.

State work-study programs.

These are similar to federal work-study programs. They usually follow the federal eligibility requirements.

AmeriCorps.

The AmeriCorps Program is designed to let students work for two years to save money for college. They are required to work 1,700 hours a year for two years. Each year they earn $4,725 plus another $7,400 in living allowances. They also receive health and child care benefits. For more information, contact the Federal Student Aid Information Center at 800-433-3243 or the White House Office of National Service, OEOB Room 145, Washington, DC 20500.

Federal internships and fellowships.

Federal money also supports a variety of internship and fellowship programs. Information is available from financial aid offices and from offices of employment and cooperative education.

College employment programs.

Colleges and universities employ students for all sorts of jobs, from washing dishes in dining halls to staffing library checkout counters to working as administrative aides in various departments. These programs are not need-based, so the jobs are open to anyone who wants them.

Some universities offer tuition remission for permanent employees who work at least half time. It can take longer to earn a degree, but you do have the advantage of a permanent job with benefits, and you can often graduate without any debt hanging over your head.

Working in the Private Sector

Students aren't limited to working on-campus or in federal, state, and college-sponsored jobs. Plenty of students work off-campus, too. They wait tables, cook in restaurants, drive taxis and buses, stock shelves, clean houses, and work at hundreds of other jobs.

Some make a lot of money. A colleague of mine has a son

who's a senior at the University of Colorado. He works as a bartender three nights a week and averages $150 a night in tips. He lives off campus with three friends and pays his own rent, utility, food, and car costs, including insurance. It has saved his parents a lot of money.

I also know a woman whose daughter put herself through school at Boston College by working as a dancer at a, ahem, gentlemen's club. On a busy night, she'd come home with $600 or $700. Her mother didn't find out about it until after her daughter had graduated (she's a successful graphic designer in New York City now, by the way). She was horrified, of course, and it took more than a few sessions with a therapist to work it through. But today, in her more pragmatic moments, she'll admit the kid was pretty shrewd.

Don't Worry about Grades

A lot of parents are concerned that having a part-time job will jeopardize their child's grades. In fact, studies have shown that a student's grades stay the same or even go up when they work 10 to 15 hours a week. They manage their time better, and they use the time devoted to study more efficiently. Many report increased self-esteem and find that they enjoy their courses more than when they weren't working. As I mentioned in an earlier chapter, my daughter works 15 hours a week behind the reception desk in her dormitory. She has a 3.72 GPA and has been on the Dean's List every semester.

POSTSCRIPT

The challenge of paying for college looms large for all American families, and the further off it is, the bigger the challenge. The decisions you make now—not next month, not next year, not five years from now—will determine how successfully you meet the challenge.

If there's one point I hope I've been able to make in this book, it's that time is your greatest ally in preparing for college. The more years you have to save and invest, the easier it will be to meet the enormous bills that await you. Likewise, the sooner you start to investigate sources of financial aid, the more successful you'll be in filling in that gap between what you have to pay and what you can afford to pay.

Start right away. Sit down with your spouse, and make a plan of action. For many people it won't be easy. Starting an investment plan will require hard work, discipline, and sacrifice. But believe me, it's worth it. And anytime you start to feel discouraged or resentful, just take a moment to look at the person whose future is at stake, and ask yourself if there's anything more important in your life. I find that always puts the whole thing into proper perspective.

Good luck.

INDEX

A

B

D

G

H

I

J

K

L

M

N

O

S

V

W